HABITS FOR A HEALTHY MARRIAGE

Richard P. Fitzgibbons, M.D.

Habits for a Healthy Marriage

A Handbook for Catholic Couples

Foreword by
Most Reverend Samuel Aquila,
Archbishop of Denver

IGNATIUS PRESS   SAN FRANCISCO

Cover art from iStock.com, Ales-A

Cover design by Riz Boncan Marsella

© 2019 by Ignatius Press, San Francisco
All rights reserved
ISBN 978-1-62164-241-1 (PB)
ISBN 978-1-64229-085-1 (eBook)
Library of Congress Control Number 2019931424
Printed in the United States of America ∞

To Saint John Paul II,
with gratitude for his luminous teaching on marriage,
and to my beloved wife, Adele,
our wonderful daughters,
my parents, John and Margaret,
and my wife's parents, John and Marie

CONTENTS

FOREWORD

A Catholic Understanding of Marriage and Family Life

By Archbishop Samuel J. Aquila, S.T.L.

A prominent Catholic psychologist in the Denver area who works with parents, children, and young adults recently told me about what she is seeing in her practice: more and more people are coming to her with serious emotional and psychological issues after they have been married for a few years.

In America, most young people do not end up on the streets, but it is common to meet teens and young adults who are going about their lives with tragically wounded hearts, even though they have a roof over their heads. Families are struggling, and the weight of their sufferings is falling particularly hard on children, who are least equipped to deal with it. Children are growing up with emotional problems that would have been uncommon only twenty-five years ago, and they still have them when they are married adults.

Many of the psychologist's clients lived together for two to three years before deciding to get married. They thought of living together as a trial run for marriage. Then, if they decided to get married in the Church, they took marriage preparation classes. When red flags were raised in the preparation process, these couples discounted them because they thought that living together made them more knowledgeable than the test or the person preparing them.

About two or three years into the marriage, however, those issues began to resurface. A wife or husband showed up in counseling, saying, "I feel as if there's a hole in my heart." The spouse had tried to fill that hole with activities, possessions, accomplishments, and pleasures, but nothing had worked.

What many couples who live together before marriage don't realize is that they began creating that "hole in their heart" when they accepted a less than full commitment as a replacement for marriage.

Every one of us is made to love others and to be loved. This truth is written into our nature. We are made in the image and likeness of God, who is love itself. So, when a couple stops short of complete self-giving in the physical, emotional, and spiritual realms, a void begins to form in their hearts.

It starts with the decision to treat the relationship casually, as something that can be tried out and discarded if it does not work out. The idea is typically couched as being prudent: "Let's try it out and see if we're really compatible. It will save us money, too."

But the physical, emotional, and spiritual messages that are sent create a much different reality. Quite often, couples who cohabit before marriage use contraception to avoid pregnancy. This sends the message "I am willing to have sex with you, but I am not willing to accept your fertility." At the emotional level, couples who live together are saying by their actions, "I like you, but I can't bring myself to commit myself to you for life." At the spiritual level, unconsciously or consciously, the message being conveyed is "I am not ready to become responsible for your holiness and to do so before God." In short, they are saying, "You are not worthy of my full commitment."

Whether or not the couple realizes or intends it, these are the messages they are communicating to each other in the unseen spiritual and emotional spheres when they decide to live together without being married.

Treating relationships as something less serious than they are is most often caused by a person's excluding God from his life or relegating him to one factor among many in making life decisions. Without God and an awareness that we are made for eternal life, relationships become consumable emotional episodes that can end at any time.

If the couple chooses to marry, they very often bring their cohabitation thinking and behaviors with them. After they're married, they frequently delay having children because it's not the "right time". Couples tell their therapist that they waited to have children because they wanted to have the money to buy a big house, a nice car, or some other material item. Spouses can also fail to give themselves completely by throwing themselves into their jobs.

With each decision to place pleasure, material things, or accomplishments above a spouse, a "contraception of the heart" occurs. Love, the selfless pouring out of oneself, is not fully given, and so it slowly begins to wilt. Then, one of the spouses has an affair and the other spouse cannot figure out why.

Sadly, children often pay the highest price for this failure to love at the deepest level. They are deprived of the security of knowing that their parents love each other fully and unconditionally, and then they feel abandoned.

One six-year-old boy went to see a counselor because he was struggling with the emotional and psychological fallout from his parents' recent divorce. In fact, he told the counselor that he wanted to kill himself and that he had a plan. When the counselor called his mother to tell her that her son was suicidal and needed her, his mother said that she could not come to pick him up because she had an important meeting. His father could not come either, because he was out of town on a business trip.

Parents and children throughout the world urgently need help. The good news is that God wants to help and has a plan for our temporal and eternal happiness. If we allow God into our lives and let him restore order, our marriages and families will become joy-filled.

The Church has received a beautiful understanding of what it means to be human. God's plan for mankind was first shown when he created Adam and Eve, and it was later elevated in Jesus Christ.

The Scriptures tell us that the very first marriage was between Adam and Eve. In Genesis, we hear, "God created man in his own image, in the image of God he created him; male and female he created them. And God blessed them, and God said to them, 'Be fruitful, and multiply'" (Gen 1:27–28). And in the second creation story we read, "Therefore a man leaves his father and his mother and clings to his wife, and they become one flesh" (Gen 2:24).

The *Catechism of the Catholic Church* explains that being made in God's image and likeness gives us the high calling of reflecting the love that exists in the Holy Trinity. The mutual love of a husband and wife "becomes an image of the absolute and unfailing love with which God loves man" (1604). But our ability to reflect God's love was damaged with the fall from grace that our first parents suffered when they chose to doubt God's goodness and love and to disobey his commands.

In these few short passages, God teaches us what marriage is: the complete, lifelong, fruitful union of a man and a woman. Saint Augustine distilled these truths into what are known as "the three goods of marriage". He described these goods as the good of children, the fidelity between the spouses, and the unbreakable bond. Each of these goods is a part of marriage because it is found in the communion of life and love that we were created to reflect—the Holy Trinity. For a union to be a true marriage, these three goods must always be respected. If they are absent, any type of relationship could be considered "marriage", and any type of sexual act could be justified.

Marriage involves not only a spiritual and emotional union but also a bodily union. This union is founded on male-female complementarity, which the book of Genesis teaches is a type of human differentiation willed by God for the benefit and fulfillment of men and women and the continuation of the human race. Children are the fruit of the bodily union of husband and wife and therefore the living reflection of their love.

What about married couples who cannot have children of their own? The Church teaches that infertility does not lessen the value of conjugal love, but she asks infertile couples to seek other ways for their love to extend beyond themselves by, for example, adopting, fostering, or educating children in need.

Defining what we mean by "family" becomes easier once we understand what marriage is. Saint John Paul II described the family as "the basic cell of society. It is the cradle of life and love, the place in which the individual 'is born' and 'grows'."[1]

We are witnessing the breakdown of many families. For children to thrive, they need to have models of masculinity and femininity, of virtue, and of selfless giving for the sake of another.

[1] Pope John Paul II, apostolic exhortation *Christifidelis Laici* (December 30, 1988), no. 40.

Sadly, too many people have believed the lies promoted by the secular culture and have constructed their lives around their own "rights". They have believed the lie that it is possible to experience the joys of total, faithful love without real self-sacrifice. No one has been hurt more by this than children, who deserve the committed, selfless love of their parents.

The solution to the wide array of issues affecting marriage and family life is not to adopt a pseudo-truth about marriage or a false pastoral approach that ends up justifying evil. The solution is fidelity to the only Truth that saves the human person: Jesus Christ! The truth is that when marriage is lived in keeping with God's plan, families become communities filled with life and love.

Even leaving God aside, the truth about marriage is seen in nature insofar as it takes a man and a woman united in the conjugal act to bring about human life. Although technological manipulation can bring about human life, it is not in the natural order and is removed from a true act of love in the total and unconditional gift of self to one's spouse. Simply and directly put, two men or two women coming together in a sexual act can never bring about a child.

There are many challenges and threats to the family today, and I realize that it is not possible for every difficult family situation to be neatly resolved. But I do know that with the grace of God and a receptive heart, every person and situation can more closely resemble the intimate exchange of love we were made to experience. I know in faith and from personal experience that hearts can be transformed and healed through an encounter with Jesus Christ. He alone can bestow on a family the peace and joy that no one can take away.

The first step in finding this peace and joy is to encounter Christ in prayer and repentance. The personal encounter with

Christ changes even the hardest heart. Thankfully, Christ has given us the Sacraments of Reconciliation, Eucharist, and Matrimony to sustain us on our journey, which is filled with our sins and shortcomings. In these sacraments, God breathes his life into us and helps us to master the powerful psychological and emotional inclinations that do great harm to marriages and children.

In the following chapters, Dr. Richard Fitzgibbons will guide you in identifying and resolving some of the major issues that are testing marriages today and might be affecting your marriage. Many of the problems that couples struggle with are rooted in the failure of their parents or even earlier generations to live in accord with God's design for marriage. And these failures have created wounds that affect spouses' ability to give themselves to their husbands and wives and to parent their children well.

In modern American society, the family must also overcome attempts to redefine marriage to include same-sex relationships, widespread acceptance of contraception, and the practice of living as though God does not exist. The Church, especially the laity, has the responsibility to proclaim the truth with joy and to invite others charitably to receive that truth.

As I write this, the Church is celebrating Easter, the greatest feast of the year. I am filled with hope for families because of Easter. I am filled with hope because all the sins of history, from Creation until the end of time, could not keep Jesus from rising from the dead. The communion of life and love that exists within the Holy Trinity is so powerful that death and sin could not conquer Christ.

And this is the mercy that God wants to pour into our wounded hearts. He wants to resurrect broken relationships through the truth, to instill courage in those afraid to commit fully, and to raise up new generations of children who are innocent and secure. So, no matter what obstacles the family faces, we can be confident that they can be overcome with God's help.

ACKNOWLEDGMENTS

I want to express my deep appreciation to many who have made this book possible, including: Saint John Paul II; Msgr. Vincent Walsh, who has synthesized and expressed in somewhat simpler language the pope's profound thoughts in *Love and Responsibility: A Simplified Version*; those in Catholic media who have allowed me to participate in shows on resolving psychological conflicts in marriages, including Johnnette Benkovic at EWTN, Drew Mariani at Relevant Radio, and Pat Coffin at Catholic Answers; Catholic Familyland, for the opportunity to give marital conferences there; Susan Wills, for her skillful and tireless work in editing the manuscript; Gail Coniglio, a truly outstanding agent and adviser; those who have supported my writing on marriage and family online at The Catholic Thing, *Homiletic and Pastoral Review*, LifeSiteNews, MercatorNet, and Aleteia; my colleagues at the Institute for Marital Healing, Dr. Peter Kleponis and our staff, especially Carolyn Defer, Maria Murphy, and Kristine Vuotto; Dr. Robert Enright, of the University of Wisconsin, coauthor of *Forgiveness Therapy*; former graduate students of the Pontifical John Paul II Institute for Studies on Marriage and Family at the Catholic University of America; and my loving and wonderfully supportive wife and reviewer, Adele. I also want to thank my publisher, Ignatius Press, and its editor Vivian Dudro; all of the Lord's priests who have offered the sacrifice of the Mass on my behalf, including Rev.

Jack Fitzgibbons, my deceased brother, Rev. Boniface von Neil, O.S.B., and Rev. John Sibel; and my friends Sr. Peggy McMahon and the late Br. Pancratius Boudreaux, C.Ss.R.

INTRODUCTION

The love which the Apostle Paul celebrates in the First Letter to the Corinthians—the love which is "patient" and "kind", and "endures all things" (1 Cor 13:4, 7)—is certainly a demanding love. *But this is precisely the source of its beauty: by the very fact that it is demanding, it builds up the true good of man and allows it to radiate to others.*

—Saint John Paul II

Love bears all things, believes all things, hopes all things, endures all things.

— 1 Corinthians 13:7

Why Another Book on Marriage?

Habits for a Healthy Marriage fulfills a strong desire I have had for many years to offer Catholic couples a book that can bring understanding and healing to their marriages. This book is meant to help couples to identify and resolve the major conflicts that weaken their relationships. It also provides a deep Catholic understanding of marriage, which is essential for strengthening marital love.

In my forty years as a psychiatrist, I have counseled hundreds of couples, families, and youth, and my professional experience has taught me that Catholic spouses can

John Paul II, Letter to Families *Gratissimam sane* (February 2, 1994), no 14. Emphasis in the original.

safeguard their marriages—and strengthen their love—by uncovering and addressing the emotional weaknesses in each of them that contribute to conflicts in their relationships. Whether you are newly engaged, recently married, or married for any number of years, the conflict-resolving strategies described in this book—the habits of a healthy marriage—can help you to protect your relationship from the emotional storms that often lead to quarrelling and mistrust, and sometimes to separation and divorce.

The Wisdom of John Paul II

Although I had excellent training in adult and child psychiatry at the hospital of the University of Pennsylvania and the Philadelphia Child Guidance Center, when I began my practice I was unprepared for the modern American problems that I encountered among my married clients. Fortunately, two years after I completed my training, John Paul II was elected pope. Four years later, his apostolic exhortation *Familiaris consortio* (On the Role of the Christian Family in the Modern World) helped me in my professional work with spouses, especially with Catholic couples. John Paul II has been called the pope of the family, and *Familiaris consortio* has been described as the Magna Carta for the family in our time.

In addition, John Paul II's book *Love and Responsibility*, written when he was bishop of Krakow, Poland, has helped me and many mental health professionals to appreciate the vital importance of working with couples on their marital self-giving, which he describes as the total surrender of one's "I" to one's spouse. This surrender is the antidote to selfishness, the greatest enemy of love, because it helps spouses to focus more on "we" and less on "me" as they become one in Christ.

Love and Responsibility also highlighted the central role of mercy in the marital relationship. Real love, as revealed to mankind by Christ, does not withdraw in the face of weakness and failure:

> The strength of such a love emerges most clearly when the beloved stumbles, when his or her weaknesses or sins come into the open. One who truly loves does not then withdraw love, but loves all the more, loves in full consciousness of the other's shortcomings and faults, and without in the least approving of them. For the person as such never loses its essential value. The emotion which attaches to the value of the person remains loyal.[1]

The pope was able to offer such helpful insights about marital love because he understood the nature of marriage.

The Nature of Marriage

There are two markedly different views about marriage. Dr. Bradford Wilcox, director of the National Marriage Project at the University of Virginia, refers to them as the older institutional model, which can be equated with the traditional Judeo-Christian view of marriage, and the newer, now more prevalent "soul-mate model".[2] In the soul-mate model, the primary obligation of marriage is not to care for one's family well but to achieve self-fulfillment through an emotionally satisfying relationship with a partner. In contrast, the Judeo-Christian understanding is that marriage

---

[1] Karol Wojtyla, *Love and Responsibility* (San Francisco: Ignatius Press, 1993), 135.

[2] W. Bradford Wilcox, "The Evolution of Divorce", *National Affairs* 37 (Fall 2018), https://www.nationalaffairs.com/publications/detail/the-evolution-of -divorce.

is a sacred, lifelong union of husband and wife with the common aims of deepening their mutual love, raising children, and helping each other to attain eternal life in God. The spouses are not preoccupied with fulfilling themselves by having a satisfying relationship in modern psychological terms but focus on becoming other Christs to each other.

To achieve this, spouses must daily attempt to grow in their ability to love as God loves, which requires ongoing personal development. This personality growth involves acknowledging one's personality weaknesses, receiving and giving forgiveness, and cultivating virtue, that is, the habits of doing good. Although this view of marriage might seem overly demanding, it is the route to true self-fulfillment.

For Catholic husbands and wives married in the Church, strength to love as Christ loves is available to them through the Sacrament of Matrimony, which is sustained by the Sacraments of Reconciliation and Eucharist. For Catholics, marriage is not a purely human institution, but one established by God, who created men and women in his own image and likeness and calls married couples to reflect his unfailing love through their lifelong fidelity to each other. This is a tall order, but the good news is that the Lord who calls also provides the grace to fulfill the calling. All couples need to do is receive that grace.

The Origins and Healing of Marital Conflicts

To receive the grace they need, couples must first recognize the weaknesses in themselves that harm their ability to love. These are acquired primarily from two sources. The first source is whichever of each spouses' parents was the most hurtful and disappointing, usually the father. The subsequent sadness, anger, mistrust, and insecurity (often referred to as "baggage") are brought unconsciously into marriage. My clinical observation of this phenomenon is supported by research demonstrating that about 70 percent of adult psychological disorders are extensions of juvenile disorders.[3] The second source of marital conflict is the hurts and the personality clashes that have occurred in the marriage. Both sources can contribute to the development of anger, selfishness, controlling behaviors, and emotional distance.

Growth in self-knowledge, in order to pinpoint marital conflicts and their causes, is a challenging process, because family-of-origin hurts are often denied or falsely thought to be caused by one's spouse. Also, people tend to put up strong walls around the pain caused by their parents. This book describes the process of uncovering the sources of conflicts and then healing them through the development of good habits, or virtues, with the help of grace. The goal of this hard work is greater trust and love, which lead to the kind of marriage that brings deep peace and lasting joy.

Uncovering the Major Conflicts

Each chapter of this book focuses on a marital conflict and a good habit, or virtue, that counteracts it. Each conflict is first illustrated in a case study. Then the conflict is identified and explained. Checklists that help to identify behaviors,

[3] J. Kim-Cohen, A. Caspi, T. E. Moffitt, H. Harrington, B. J. Milne, and R. Poulton, "Prior Juvenile Diagnoses in Adults with Mental Disorder", *Archives of General Psychiatry* 60, no. 7 (2003): 709–17, https://doi.org/10.1001/archpsyc.60.7.709.

emotional responses, thoughts, and communication styles that point to the presence of conflicts are provided.

Underlying each chapter is the recognition that the emotional weaknesses causing marital stress are often hidden. Most spouses do not deliberately set out to hurt the persons they have vowed to honor and love all the days of their lives. Instead, they unconsciously inflict painful wounds because of injuries suffered in the past. Sadly, if the conflicts are not uncovered and addressed, spouses can turn in on themselves and surrender to hopelessness. The good news is that marital conflicts can be correctly identified and, in many cases, resolved, especially if there is a faith component in the healing process, as described in this book.

Who Should Read This Book

Singles

By providing knowledge of how the most common relationship stresses can be uncovered and resolved, this book can help Catholic singles to be more hopeful about becoming successful Catholic spouses. Catholic singles need more confidence and positive views about marriage, particularly in view of the clear withdrawal from commitment to marriage that has been occurring in the past forty-five years.

The dramatic fall in Catholic marriage rates has been observed by the Center for Applied Research in the Apostolate (CARA) at Georgetown University. CARA reported 426,309 Catholic marriages in 1969, 261,626 marriages in 2000, and 144,148 in 2016.[4] In 2014, the Bureau of Labor Statistics reported that 49.8 percent of adults in the United States were married, compared with 62.6 percent in 1976.

---

[4] Center for Applied Research in the Apostolate, *Frequently Requested Church Statistics*, https://cara.georgetown.edu/frequently-requested-church-statistics/.

The most important chapter of this book for singles is the one on selfishness, because selfishness is so widespread and is a major reason for the retreat from marriage. If this conflict is identified in a dating relationship, it can be discussed as described in chapter 2.

Engaged Couples

Engaged couples will especially benefit from reading and completing the self-knowledge questions in chapter 12. This chapter identifies weaknesses acquired from family of origin, peers, or previous loving relationships that can emerge at any time and can harm marriages. The stories of many couples in this book demonstrate how these vulnerabilities can be uncovered, discussed, and resolved.

Engaged couples who identify in their relationship specific personality conflicts caused by anger, selfishness, or controlling, emotionally distant, and anxious behaviors should read and discuss the chapters related to those issues. They should also read the communication chapter to identify the most loving and respectful way to discuss those behaviors.

Engaged persons who have been traumatized by their parents' divorce need to understand how this experience can damage their ability to trust in marriage. Difficulties with trust have been described as the legacy of divorce. Unless a process of building and protecting trust is initiated, serious marital difficulties could arise for children of divorced parents. These young men and women can benefit from the chapters on anxiety and divorce prevention.

Parents

This book can assist parents, who have the primary responsibility for the long-term preparation of their children for marriage. Parents can do this most effectively by modeling a loving, sacrificially giving, cheerful Catholic marriage and by communicating the Church's truth about marriage. They can also prepare their children for their future marriages by correcting their selfish tendencies when they are young. For this task, parents can benefit from the chapter on selfishness, which will help them understand this leading enemy of marital and family love.

Bishops and Priests

This book can assist bishops and priests in their indispensable role of preaching the truth about the Sacrament of Matrimony and Catholic family life. It can strengthen them in their vital ministry to couples, helping them to communicate with greater confidence that, with the Lord's help, most marital conflicts can be uncovered and resolved.

Priests can use this book as a resource for parishioners who turn to them with their marital troubles and can refer couples to the chapters that address their conflicts. Both bishops and priests would benefit from reading the chapter on divorce prevention, which stresses the importance of self-knowledge in each spouse with regard to family-of-origin and marital weaknesses as well as previous hurts in loving relationships.

In a culture that manifests increasing hostility toward the Church's teaching on sexual morality and marriage, the chapter on resolving self-esteem weaknesses and strengthening confidence can embolden clergy to communicate without fear the much-needed truth in these areas.

Although they are not married, bishops and priests can benefit personally from this book. Priests and married couples often struggle with the same issues that stem from their families of origin as they strive to give themselves completely to the Lord in accordance with their vocation.

The habits needed for a healthy marriage are also needed for a healthy priesthood.

Vocation directors can be assisted in their evaluation of candidates for the priesthood and religious life by the last chapter, on parental legacies. This important knowledge could lead them to request that the mental health professionals who do testing on candidates identify the predominant psychological weakness from each candidate's family background, as well as his psychological strengths. Significant weaknesses could be addressed before and during formation.

Mental Health Professionals

This book can help mental health professionals who desire to assist Catholic couples in identifying their predominant family-of-origin psychological weakness and in making a commitment to engage in the hard work of mastering them. Without this work, and the giving and receiving of forgiveness, a deep healing process cannot begin. The result can be the often-heard complaint that marital therapy seems only to help spouses through divorce. A major study of six hundred couples highlighted the pitfalls of current marital therapy: those who received marital counseling were two to three times more likely to divorce than couples who did not have counseling.[5]

The personal journey toward forgiveness is very important for mental health professionals themselves. Their own work of forgiveness for hurts in secure attachment relationships is essential to their ability to offer effective marital therapy. Only after they practice forgiveness and

---

[5] Steven L. Nock, Laura Ann Sanchez, and James D. Wright, *Covenant Marriage: The Movement to Reclaim Tradition in America* (New Brunswick, N.J.: Rutgers University Press, 2008), 112.

overcome their resentments are they are in the best position to assist couples in practicing forgiveness.

Catholic Spouses

Spouses do not have to read this book from start to finish. Rather, one or both might benefit from reading those chapters that describe their most troubling issues. In view of the prevalence of selfishness in the culture and the serious harm it causes, however, I recommend that all spouses read the chapter on selfishness. In addition, I recommend the material in chapter 12, on growth in self-knowledge.

By engaging in the hard work suggested in this book, Catholic spouses can experience a deeper understanding of their marriage, a resolution of their major conflicts, and an improvement in their marital friendship and love. They do not need to seek professional marital therapy. In fact, research cited in the divorce prevention chapter demonstrates that mental health professionals do not have a particularly good track record in helping troubled marriages. A valid criticism is that counseling for seriously troubled marriages often focuses more on pleasing an unhappy spouse and on facilitating a divorce than on trying to uncover each spouse's weaknesses and working to save the marriage.

Marital friendship, trust, and love that have weakened or grown cold can be surprisingly and delightfully strengthened and renewed. The process for this to happen is challenging but rewarding. By growing in the humility of self-knowledge and by practicing virtues with the help of grace, the flame of marital love can be relit and burn stronger than before.

Forgiveness Reduces Anger

Forgiveness is above all a personal choice, a decision of the heart to go against the natural instinct to pay back evil with evil.

—Saint John Paul II

Then Peter came up and said to him, "Lord, how often shall my brother sin against me, and I forgive him? As many as seven times?" Jesus said to him, "I do not say to you seven times, but seventy times seven."

—Matthew 18:21–22

This chapter explains the benefits of forgiveness in reducing and resolving anger from immediate stressful events, from past hurts in a marriage, and from unrecognized hurts from one's youth. Daily forgiveness protects marriages from the damaging effects of excessive anger.

Outbursts of anger can harm one's spouse and children. Mature adults should be able to master their anger even if learning how to avoid overreacting entails hard work. Mastering anger involves using forgiveness to uncover and to resolve the pain that spouses have brought unconsciously into their marriages, most often from their relationships with parents or from previous loving relationships.

John Paul II, Message for World Day of Peace (January 1, 2002), no. 8.

Deeply buried anger over past hurts that has developed over the course of many years is a leading enemy of marital love, because it is regularly misdirected unintentionally at one's spouse. The good news is that forgiveness therapy resolves anger from the present and the past, thereby protecting spouses and children from harmful overreactions.

Scott and Monica

Scott's jaw showed the unmistakable sign of clenched teeth as he entered my office. Behind Monica's forced smile, her eyes were cold. When they sat down, their stiffness and discomfort were clearly apparent.

"Monica says I'm always mad," Scott began, "but if she would just be a little more understanding—"

"Me?" Monica interrupted. "I'm not the one shouting and screaming and carrying on all the time."

"If you would just treat me with more respect and listen to me, I wouldn't have to raise my voice to get your attention." Scott's voice grew louder and his face redder.

"I might be able to figure out what you want if you weren't yelling at me day and night," Monica replied.

I quickly called a time-out.

Scott and Monica obviously had difficulties with excessive anger. After a few probing questions, it was clear that Scott reacted to any perceived slight with intense anger. In her turn, Monica withdrew and gave Scott the cold shoulder. They would reconcile for a time, but soon the pattern would repeat itself. Anger was seriously harming their marriage and diminishing the strong love they had for each other.

Over the next few sessions, as they worked at trying to understand the origins of their difficulties, they realized that neither one intended to hurt the other. They did harm to each other because they lacked knowledge about their emotional weaknesses and did not understand how to master their anger. They slowly came to recognize that they had each carried into their marriage significant unresolved anger from their families of origin, which contributed to their overreactions. Scott's father was emotionally distant, and Monica's father had been an alcoholic. Both fathers struggled with their tempers and frequently overreacted in direct and passive anger.

Scott's and Monica's anger diminished through a process of uncovering and resolving buried anger by growing in the habit of forgiveness. Practicing forgiveness did not come naturally or easily for them; it required hard work. Scott and Monica were pleased, however, that their efforts resulted in numerous benefits. For instance, they grew in their ability to resolve both childhood anger and anger arising from the numerous challenges in married life. Also, as they overcame their anger, their hearts opened more, and they rediscovered stronger love for each other.

The Nature of Anger

Anger is a strong feeling of displeasure and antagonism, most often aroused by a sense of injury or wrong. It is a natural response to the failure of others to meet one's needs for love, respect, and praise. Excessive anger can be the result of selfishness, anxiety, sadness, or modeling after an angry parent.

Anger is usually present when there are conflicts in relationships, whether at home, at school, at work, or in the community. Being angry or dealing with an angry person can be a daily experience for many people. In a study of 1,300 psychiatric outpatients, one half had moderate to severe anger, which was comparable with their levels of anxiety and depression.[1]

When a person is hurt by another, he first experiences sadness, followed by anger. This anger can then encompass the sadness and the anger from the past, causing a person to overreact to the present situation and making it more difficult to resolve. Saint John Paul II warned that, without forgiveness, one could be a prisoner of past anger. People usually tend to think of their anger as justifiable and appropriate. Excessive anger, however, is neither of those things, especially if it punishes people in the present for injuries done by others in the past.

The Damage Caused by Anger

The obvious damage caused by anger is the emotional and physical harm inflicted on those at the receiving end of a person's wrath. Not surprisingly, studies have found a tenfold increased risk for depressive symptoms in those living with an angry spouse. People are hardwired to receive love, respect, and sensitivity, not bitterness, from others. Anger directed at spouses increases their anxiety, lowers their ability to trust, weakens their confidence, increases their irritability, and can harm their physical health.

The children of angry people also suffer harm. Children crave a feeling of safety in the home, which is dependent on their parents' stable union. Quarreling between their parents causes children to suffer sadness, anger, anxiety,

[1] Michael A. Posternak and Mark Zimmerman, "Anger and Aggression in Psychiatric Outpatients", *Journal of Clinical Psychiatry* 63, no. 8 (2002): 665–72, http://dx.doi.org/10.4088/JCP.v63n0803.

insecurity, and fears about the possibility of separation or divorce. It might cause children to feel guilty, wondering if they contributed to their parents' anger, or to develop physical illnesses, including irritable bowel syndrome, or psychological illnesses, such as anxiety or obsessive-compulsive disorders.

Less obvious is the harm anger does to the angry person himself. Although anger in its early stages is often associated with the sadness caused by being hurt, it can later be associated with the pleasure derived from its expression. This ugly phenomenon is often seen in a person who, when young, feared his father yet never expressed anger at him but later finds pleasure in expressing anger at his spouse or at someone else. The enjoyment of angry feelings and of the high associated with its arousal and release can become a serious psychological and spiritual disorder. It can also become a danger to one's physical health. A Harvard Medical School study found a more than two-fold greater risk of heart attack after an outburst of anger. The greater the intensity of the outburst, the greater the risk.[2] Clearly, mastery over anger is essential to health and well-being.

The Origins of Anger

Anger can begin in early childhood and later extend into relationships with those whom one wants to trust with one's heart. Anger over the harm done by parents and

[2] E. Mostofsky, M. Maclure, G.H. Tofler, J.E. Muller, M.A. Mittleman, "Relation of Outbursts of Anger and Risk of Acute Myocardial Infarction", *American Journal of Cardiology* 112, no. 3 (August 1, 2013): 343–48, https://doi.org/10.1016/j.amjcard.2013.03.035.

others can lie buried for years or even decades and then emerge in one's marriage, where it is misdirected at the person one loves most, one's spouse.

Anger can arise from disappointments and stresses in a marriage itself. In a spousal relationship, anger can originate from loneliness, lack of affection, poor communication, selfish and controlling behaviors, and anxiety. Anger can also be caused by excessive feelings of responsibility, work stress, lack of balance in one's life, jealousy, conflicts with in-laws, inappropriate expectations, substance abuse, defiant behaviors in children, financial worries, lack of sleep, and illness, whether one's own or a family member's. Pride can be a source of excessive anger, leading spouses to overreact to minor stresses and mishaps. Mastering pride requires growing in the virtues of meekness and humility. Lastly, some spouses are surprised to discover that the origin of their anger is post-abortion trauma.

Three Methods of Dealing with Anger

Sometimes anger is a signal that arouses a person to do something about an injustice. Take, for example, a person who witnesses a man stealing a woman's purse. The bystander's anger is the proper response to the situation, and it stimulates him to pursue the thief (while calling the police, of course).

Most of the anger people experience within marriage, however, is aroused not by real injustices but by minor stresses and mishaps. When anger develops from something of this sort, there are three basic options for dealing with this complex and powerful emotion: (1) deny it, (2) express it actively or passively, or (3) forgive the perceived injury. Forgiveness is the most effective way to reduce and to master anger in married life. It alone can resolve the anger from past disappointments with others that most spouses unconsciously bring into marriage.

Denial

During childhood, the most common psychological method for dealing with anger is denial, which for many people continues into adult life. The reasons for denial are numerous and include the need to idealize one's parents, siblings, or peers; a lack of knowledge about how to resolve anger with forgiveness; fears and insecurities about expressing anger; a sense of shame; a fear of sadness associated with anger; a desire to maintain a peaceful and loving home life; and loyalty to parents. For a child, the relationship in which anger is denied the most is his relationship with his father. The major reasons for this are the fear of an angry response from his father or the fear that a greater distance from him will develop.

As time passes, the dangers of relying on denial to cope with anger include sadness, anxiety, insecurity, and even an increase of the very anger that is being denied. The failure to admit and to resolve one's anger can lead to its being misdirected at siblings, parents, peers, and eventually one's spouse and children. This psychological dynamic is a major cause of overreactive anger in married life.

The major way to overcome denial is not the one most often recommended—that is, to express anger at others. This creates more tension for the angry person and those around him. There is a much greater benefit in thinking, "I want to overcome the possibility that I am in denial by exploring the need to forgive. Do I need to forgive a parent, a sibling, or a peer who hurt me in the past? Do I need to forgive my spouse right now?"

Expression

Unfortunately, many spouses believe that the best way to deal with anger is to express it. Some are encouraged by the psychologically unproven opinion that letting off steam is healthy. They are regularly supported in this approach to anger by family, friends, self-help literature, and even a good number of mental health professionals. They fail to realize, however, the serious risks involved in giving vent to their angry feelings.

The psychological reality is that most spouses do not know how to express anger fairly, because they have brought so much buried unconscious anger into their marriages. Most husbands and wives don't realize that receiving anger from the person whom they trust and love most in their lives can leave deep wounds. Every time anger is expressed between spouses, trust decreases, and subsequently feelings of love also diminish. The expression of anger does not fully resolve this emotion and does not help to resolve marital conflicts.

The use of forgiveness, however, does resolve anger from both present and past hurts, thereby diminishing marital stress. It helps to eliminate angry outbursts. The path to forgiveness begins with identifying the ways anger is expressed, either directly and honestly or indirectly, in a passive-aggressive, or masked, manner. The following list can help to identify the types of active and passive-aggressive anger in a marriage:

Active
- Disrespectfulness
- Excessive quarreling
- Irritability
- Frequent frustration

- Being easily annoyed
- Negative communication and criticism
- Rudeness

Passive-Aggressive
- Silent, cold treatment
- Irresponsible behaviors
- Withholding affection and expressions of love
- Deliberate sloppiness, lack of care for the home or oneself
- Uncooperative behavior
- Lack of support

After identifying the ways anger is expressed in a marriage, spouses can move on to the best method for dealing with this emotion: forgiveness.

Forgiveness

Forgiveness involves uncovering anger from one's family of origin, from past relationships, and from one's marriage and then deciding to work on letting go of this anger without misdirecting it at one's spouse, children, or others. It also involves choosing to forgive immediately the person in the present who has aroused one's anger. Forgiveness therapy is a psychologically proven method for diminishing and resolving the damage caused by excessive anger.[3]

Forgiveness can produce many benefits. It can help individuals forget past painful experiences and free them

[3] For a presentation of the research on forgiveness therapy and its methods, see Robert D. Enright and Richard P. Fitzgibbons, *Forgiveness Therapy: An Empirical Guide for Resolving Anger and Restoring Hope* (Washington, D.C.: American Psychological Association, 2014).

from the subtle control of people and events associated with these events. It can facilitate reconciliation between spouses and between them and other family members. And it can decrease the likelihood that anger will be misdirected in the home. My colleague Dr. Robert Enright has demonstrated through numerous studies at the University of Wisconsin–Madison what we see daily in clinical practice: forgiveness enhances confidence and helps to resolve feelings of sadness and anxiety.[4] It can also prevent the recurrence of these feelings.

The Process of Forgiveness

Although forgiveness is the most effective method for gaining control over the strong emotion of anger, it does not come naturally or easily. After uncovering the deepest origins of anger, which are often denied or unconscious, and trying to understand the life journey and past relationships of the person who has inflicted the hurt, there is still the work of forgiveness itself.

The first step in the process of forgiveness is for both spouses to identify their childhood experiences of being hurt by parents or others. Each spouse needs to identify the parent who disappointed him more. Next, it is helpful for each spouse to try to understand the other spouse's parental relationships. As this uncovering work proceeds, couples develop the awareness that a spouse's behaviors can most often be attributed to past emotional hurts from parents or others or to modeling after and repeating a parent's personality weaknesses. Looking at the past to understand the present usually leads to the realization that people

[4] Ibid.

often do not deliberately inflict hurt. Even people who are deliberately cruel have often suffered some sort of trauma early in life.

After both spouses achieve a certain amount of self-knowledge and knowledge of the other, the work of forgiveness can begin. This work can occur in one of three ways: with one's mind (cognitively), from one's heart (emotionally), or in prayer (spiritually).

Cognitive Forgiveness with the Mind

The work of forgiveness begins by making a resolution to stop expressing anger toward one's spouse and children. How? By resolving, when upset, to think about forgiving before even speaking, to think immediately, "I want to understand and forgive, understand and forgive, understand and forgive." As one repeats these words in his mind, his anger begins to diminish. We call this an immediate forgiveness exercise. At times, while engaging in this exercise, a painful memory can emerge involving someone else. One can then shift his thoughts to forgiving that person also.

When anger decreases through this practice, people are better able to communicate with each other. As spouses tell each other more clearly and easily what they really need from each other, they can discuss dispassionately what the situation at hand really requires.

Emotional Forgiveness from the Heart

With emotional forgiveness, someone truly feels like forgiving the person who has hurt him. It is usually preceded by the hard work of forgiving with one's mind. As anger decreases, through the cognitive strategy described above, the basic goodness of the offending person is usually seen more clearly. As one better understands the other, compassion grows.

Stronger feelings of love and trust grow between spouses when they cease to be controlled by emotional pain from the past. As they learn to master their anger, they also usually become less anxious and more confident and thus better able to offer gentle, not angry, responses to family members in need of correction.

Some spouses feel guilty about not having feelings of forgiveness right away. They believe that, as Christians, they should forgive from the heart immediately. They may even think they are not truly forgiving if they do not feel like forgiving. Spouses need to be aware that forgiveness from the heart can take a long time, even years, and that, in the interim, cognitive forgiveness is effective and sincere. If people have difficulty with emotionally forgiving their spouses, parents, or others who have harmed them, they need not become discouraged.

Forgiveness from the heart is the most profound level of forgiveness. It is achieved through a deep understanding of an offender's weaknesses and his childhood. This knowledge regularly leads to an attitude of compassion toward the offender. In time, one can truly feel like forgiving the offender with a generous heart. This end point is often reached, however, only after a long journey of forgiving with one's mind or with prayer, which is the third method of forgiveness.

Spiritual Forgiveness in Prayer

Exercising the theological virtue of faith through prayer can be effective in diminishing excessive anger in marriages. Some hurts from childhood or marriage are so severe and painful that a spouse may have difficulty initiating forgiveness either with the mind or the heart. There can be times in the healing process when forgiveness seems impossible, as commonly happens if hurts by a spouse or by a parent or an in-law are ongoing.

Often one spouse can be engaged in the forgiveness process while the other spouse continues with the offending behaviors. During such times, spiritual forgiveness can be effective in diminishing anger. This can occur in a number of ways, including recognizing that one is powerless over one's anger and deciding to turn it over to God, praying, "Lord, take my anger" or "Lord, forgive [my spouse, my parent, or some other person], for I can't at this time." Catholics can also take their struggle with forgiveness to the Sacrament of Reconciliation. As with cognitive and emotive forgiveness, spiritual forgiveness may need to be done repeatedly before strong anger diminishes and over-reactions cease. Overcoming anger can take time.

Daily Forgiveness

The Lord told Saint Peter to forgive not seven times but seventy times seven times, meaning many times each day. This is psychologically necessary because hurts and disappointments happen all the time. It is helpful to follow Saint Paul's advice: "Do not let the sun go down on your anger" (Eph 4:26). One can do this by reflecting at bedtime on one's behavior that day, by asking God for forgiveness, and by forgiving others in turn.

Misconceptions and Obstacles to Forgiveness

Sometimes the decision to forgive is difficult to make because of a deep-seated desire for justice. Some are reluctant to forgive because they think that the decision to do so denies the seriousness of the injury or somehow excuses the offender. Another common misconception that blocks forgiveness is the idea that the offender must apologize first.

Forgiveness does not require an apology or even a belief that the offender will change his behavior. But forgiveness also does not require trusting an offender who does not demonstrate a desire to change. Forgiveness does, on the other hand, make one stronger in facing and addressing hurts and in offering appropriate correction to offenders when necessary. Some people mistakenly think that forgiveness is a sign of weakness, but, in fact, it is an indication of a healthy, strong personality.

Fear that sadness associated with past hurts could emerge and be overwhelming is another obstacle to forgiveness. Although forgiveness can result initially in the emergence of some unresolved sadness and anger, these will decrease as the inner strength that grows from forgiveness increases self-esteem. Both Dr. Enright's research studies at the University of Wisconsin and our clinical experience demonstrate that unresolved emotional conflicts diminish with forgiveness.

Immediate Forgiveness Exercises

Spouses need to learn how to address anger quickly whenever it happens in response to daily stresses in the home and at work. A prompt forgiveness process is essential to marital happiness, family stability, and the psychological health of spouses and children.

The sharp words of an angry person can be as painful as a slap across the face, especially for sensitive people. Whereas physical anger harms the body, verbal anger can wound the heart, which can be far more difficult to heal, as the book of Sirach suggests: "Any wound, but not a wound of the heart!" (25:13). Anger can also be expressed in passive-aggressive ways, such as coldness or the silent treatment, which harms marriages and parent-child relationships as well.

Just as a serious infectious disease needs prompt treatment, so, too, anger needs the immediate remedy of forgiveness to protect the health of spouses and children. The failure to admit and to resolve anger through immediate forgiveness creates excessive tension, harms marital love and trust, and causes fear, mistrust, and sadness in children. A desire to protect their children from the harmful and frightening aspects of their anger can motivate many parents to work on mastering their anger as quickly as they can.

Instead of giving in to anger when under emotional stress, spouses and parents should inwardly repeat phrases such as the following: "Forgive, forgive, forgive"; "I want to understand and forgive"; "I want to be loyal to the goodness in my spouse [or my child] and forgive"; "Lord, take my anger." These phrases come more easily when a husband or a wife knows that the other spouse is also working hard to change insensitive behaviors.

When a person loses his temper, he should immediately identify the cause of his anger, apologize to the person at the receiving end of his anger, and commit or recommit to mastering his anger by forgiving the person whose behavior provoked the angry response. The unwillingness to take these steps and to make progress in mastering anger is a serious psychological weakness and a leading reason for severe marital conflicts, separation, and even divorce.

This weakness is encouraged by our narcissistic culture, which enables adults to act immaturely and with an attitude of entitlement by erupting in anger when things do not go exactly their way or by withholding love and cooperation from people who have slighted them. The commitment to struggle against these forms of selfishness is essential to mastering anger.

The reason behind anger is often the unconscious modeling after an angry, controlling, or selfish parent. When such a pattern is identified, spouses can immediately ask the Lord to help them to repeat the good qualities of their parents but not their weaknesses, so that the spouses can fulfill their marital vows to cherish and honor each other. At that moment, they can forgive the parents whose anger might have hurt them deeply and who set a bad example.

Past Forgiveness Exercises

Every spouse brings into his marriage some (usually unconscious) hurts and disappointments from his family background or previous relationships. These hurts can cast a dark cloud over a marriage and undermine one's ability to give oneself lovingly, gently, cheerfully, and respectfully to one's spouse. Uncovering and resolving such conflicts, which are often associated with significant amounts of anger, are essential for maintaining a healthy personality and, subsequently, a fulfilling marriage. In fact, without forgiveness, a spouse will continue to be controlled to some extent by past offenders and plagued by sadness, anger, mistrust, and insecurity associated with past hurts.

The use of past forgiveness exercises brings a greater freedom to love fully. Here is how to use past forgiveness exercises for anger in marriage. After uncovering family-of-origin hurts, the spouse imagines himself as a child or a teenager, saying, "Dad [or Mom], I want to understand your childhood with your parents and to forgive you for the hurts of the past." The result of this exercise, when used regularly, is that overall angry responses decrease, and the spouse acts less often like the angry parent.

Anger from severe childhood hurts due to a parent's selfishness, substance abuse, controlling behavior, neglect, or anger is not resolved quickly, nor is anger over abandonment by one's parents or their divorce. One who has had a stressful relationship with a parent must practice past forgiveness exercises regularly, even for many years, to prevent anger toward the parent from being misdirected at one's spouse. Spouses can encourage one another in these exercises, and they can pray for their parents and other relatives.

The use of past forgiveness exercises can result in the emergence of strong, previously buried feelings of anger from childhood hurts. For a time, this old anger can feel intense and bring with it sadness or anxiety. This pain will diminish, however, as the spouse perseveres in working on understanding and forgiving those who caused him harm.

A major challenge in the healing process is encountered when one tries to forgive a parent who was emotionally or physically abusive. Taking the intense anger that one feels toward such a parent to the Sacrament of Reconciliation can help. For many spouses, the resolution of severe childhood betrayals can be so difficult that the process of forgiveness may need to continue periodically for the rest of their lives.

In some marriages, the major hurts from the family background were inflicted by a brother or a sister whose anger at a parent or someone else was misdirected at a sibling. Wrath that sprang from unchecked jealousy and rivalry can also leave deep wounds. Saint Thomas Aquinas described jealousy as the "mother of hatred". Cain slew his brother Abel because he was jealous of him (see Gen 4:3–8). A spouse who was injured by a sibling may find it beneficial to reflect, "I want to understand why my brother [or sister] overreacted in anger at me. I want to forgive him so that I don't misdirect anger meant for him at my spouse." In addition to forgiving the sibling, a person might need to correct ongoing insensitive and offending behaviors.

Unresolved Father Anger in Husbands

The father relationship is the most common source of unresolved anger from the family background. The process of forgiving his father can be challenging for a man, because most men have never discussed with anyone their disappointment with their fathers. Instead of identifying and addressing emotional conflicts, such as excessive anger, men tend to employ significant denial.

When hurts are uncovered in men, the failure of a father to be emotionally supportive and affirming is the one most commonly expressed. When a man attempts to understand his father, he usually discovers that when his father had been a child, he lacked a close relationship with his father. This knowledge usually results in compassion for the father and a desire to forgive him. Identifying and being thankful for a father's good qualities, such as loyalty, fidelity, strength, and faith, facilitate the forgiveness process. Marital healing is also helped when husbands who have misdirected father anger at their wives and children ask for their family's forgiveness and commit themselves to mastering such anger.

An obstacle to asking for forgiveness is the pleasure a person can experience in venting anger. As stated earlier, anger in its early stages is most often associated with the sadness of hurt, but later it can be associated with pleasure in its expression, even though the recipient, a wife, does not deserve it. If they are aware that they are at the receiving end of misdirected anger, wives should not hold back in encouraging their husbands to engage in the hard work of forgiving their fathers.

Unresolved Father Anger in Wives

The most common causes of father hurts in a woman are her father's anger, emotional distance, selfishness, controlling behavior, substance abuse, or infidelity. A father's lack of sensitivity toward her mother also contributes to a woman's sense of injury. If her parents divorced, she is likely to hold this against her father.

Under stress, this unconscious anger can be misdirected at a husband. Unless such anger with fathers is uncovered and addressed through a lengthy and demanding forgiveness process, the wife and the marriage can be seriously harmed by the behaviors of the offending father. Expressing anger toward the father for painful hurts of the past, which therapists often recommend, does not resolve such anger. Anger is resolved only through a forgiveness process.

The failure to resolve father anger can prompt a wife to behave as though her husband has the same serious emotional or character weaknesses as her offending father. The anger and the mistrust she felt toward her father can be misdirected at her husband in active ways, such as being overly critical and disrespectful, or in passive-aggressive ways, such as refusing to show affection, failing to care for the home, or undermining her husband's relationships with their children, which is referred to as "paternal alienation". Some wives mentally conflate their offending fathers with their basically trustworthy husbands to such an extent that they demand a separation or a divorce. In such a case, it is essential that family members and spouses speak honestly about the deep father wound so that it does not cause further harm to the marriage and the children.

Some wives who never expressed anger with a difficult father can find pleasure in later misdirecting this anger toward their husbands. When this is uncovered, initially most wives will deny doing this and may even claim that at a certain time in the past they completely forgave their fathers for all the hurts of their youth. The psychological reality is that resolving anger from childhood requires periodic ongoing forgiveness for years and often decades. Ironically, the failure of a wife to forgive an angry father can lead to her repeating his psychologically harmful behaviors in marriage.

A husband who is aware of his wife's father wounds should not be afraid to ask her to try to overcome her anger and mistrust by engaging in the hard work of forgiving her father. By meditating on trusting the Lord with the marriage, the husband can find the courage he needs to make an appropriate, loving correction.

Unresolved Mother Anger in Husbands

Husbands who had insensitive, controlling, addicted, depressed, or selfish mothers regularly overreact in anger meant for their mothers at the persons they love most in their lives, their wives. These husbands often use anger to keep their wives at a distance because of a deeply rooted, unconscious fear of being hurt or controlled by them, as they and their fathers had been controlled by their mothers.

Many such husbands go to great lengths to be out of the home, which is an unconscious repetition of their child-hood behavior to avoid their controlling mothers.

Husbands can resolve these mother wounds by making a daily commitment to understand and to forgive their mothers for their controlling behaviors toward them and their fathers. In this process, they often discover that their mothers either never felt safe or were repeating the con-trolling behaviors present in one of their parents. It is also essential for a husband mentally to separate his wife from his insensitive mother by daily reflecting on the fact that his wife is sensitive and trustworthy.

Husbands with emotionally insensitive mothers often struggle with strong anger toward their fathers for failing to protect them from the mothers' offending behaviors. Engaging in the forgiveness process toward their fathers is an essential aspect of resolving this serious obstacle to marital love.

The wife who is on the receiving end of misdirected mother anger should consider identifying the true source of her husband's anger and possibly request that her husband work on forgiving his mother. Wives regularly victimized by misdirected anger experience a loss of trust and a subse-quent loss of loving feelings for their husbands, which may lead them to consider separation or even divorce.

Unresolved Mother Anger in Wives

Women tend to be more fortunate emotionally than men in that they usually have received much more praise and affirmation from their role models (their mothers) than men receive from their role models (their fathers). A small, but growing number of wives, however, report being deeply disappointed by mothers who gave in to the narcissistic, contraceptive, and materialistic trends in modern society. These once neglected girls, now women, can overreact in irritability under the normal stresses of married and family life because they did not experience enough comforting maternal love as children and teenagers. At times, they can resent giving praise and love because they received so little maternal affirmation. Under various types of stress, they may misdirect anger meant for their mothers at their husbands, children, and others.

The process of forgiving an insensitive mother is challenging for a woman, because the mother's behavior seemed so unnatural. An uncaring mother does not reflect the feminine nurturing role children naturally need and expect. Fortunately, daughters of insensitive mothers often have a comforting grandmother or are close to the mothers of their girlfriends.

The most effective way to forgive in this case is with spiritual forgiveness, in which a woman realizes that she is powerless over her anger and wants to turn it over to God, or she asks God to forgive her mother. Catholic women relate that they have found comfort and healing by meditating on the Virgin Mary's loving presence in their lives.

Encouraging Past Forgiveness Exercises

If spouses believe that their husbands or wives misdirect anger at them due to a failure to resolve anger with a parent or with another person from their past, they should not be afraid to express this view in a gentle, compassionate manner. One could state, "Honey, I believe our marriage would be helped if you thought about forgiving your father [or mother] for the ways in which you were hurt when you were young or are being hurt now." The fact is, past forgiveness exercises contribute effectively to the strengthening of marital friendship and to the reconciliation of spouses by powerfully removing anger. Without their use, marital conflicts are often not resolved. Rather, they become recurrent because of locked-in resentment and entrenched patterns of behavior.

The Truth about Self-Forgiveness

When one has inflicted a hurt upon a spouse, a child, a loved one, or others, the appropriate psychological responses are to apologize, to ask for forgiveness, and to make a commitment to change so that offending words, behaviors, or deeds are not repeated. An offending spouse should also identify the origin of his weaknesses and decide to work on growing in the virtues needed to resolve it. A similar dynamic occurs in the Sacrament of Reconciliation, in which one confesses a sin, makes a firm purpose of amendment not to repeat it, and experiences the relief of being forgiven. The feelings of guilt that arise from hurting someone decrease when one commits to change and is forgiven.

Feelings of guilt do not decrease when a spouse thinks, "I forgive myself. That's all that matters." In fact, self-forgiveness fosters the major enemy of marital love—selfishness.[5] It minimizes both the harm one has inflicted and the need one has to be forgiven by God and others. Guilty feelings linger because a true reconciliation has not taken place. Marital stress continues for the same reason.

[5] Paul Vitz and J.M. Meade, "Self-Forgiveness in Psychology and Psychotherapy", *Journal of Religion and Health* 50, no. 2 (June 2011): 248–63.

Post-abortion Anger and Forgiveness

Post-abortion sadness, anger, mistrust, and guilt are psychological conflicts that some spouses present in the course of marital therapy. Not infrequently, a wife harbors strong anger at her husband for feeling that he pressured her into obtaining an abortion. In many of these marriages, the husbands have admitted that they made a terrible mistake and have asked for forgiveness. The periodic intense anger that continues to emerge in the wives illustrates that the work of forgiveness for abortion trauma has to go on for many years. Spouses report being greatly helped by taking the post-abortion pain to the Sacrament of Reconciliation. Also, participation in post-abortion healing programs, such as Project Rachel, has helped many spouses.

Post-abortion mistrust, sadness, and anger are often unconscious. A priest told me that when couples ask him for counseling because of excessive anger, he often asks if there has been an abortion in their past. He related that the answer to this question is often yes. When I posed this question to a man who came to me exhausted by the amount of strife between him and his wife, he raised one finger and bowed his head. Shortly thereafter, he told his wife that he believed their abortion had severely harmed each of them and had been a hidden source of conflict in their relationship. He asked forgiveness for his role in the abortion and recommended that they both confess the sin in the Sacrament of Reconciliation.

The Benefits of Faith

For over forty years as a psychiatrist, I have seen that many Catholic couples who struggle with anger are greatly helped by their faith. Prayer and the sacraments, especially the Eucharist and Reconciliation, help spouses to deal with anger from the past and the present in a more mature, rational, loving manner. Also helpful is meditating on Scripture and taking to heart these words of Saint Paul: "Husbands, love your wives, and do not be harsh with them" (Col 3:19), and "Let the wife see that she respects her husband" (Eph 5:33).

Forgiveness is the key to overcoming anger. In the succeeding chapters, we will return to the use of forgiveness therapy to resolve the anger that can be associated with other marital conflicts. Faith will be further revealed as a tremendous source of support for couples striving to grow in Christlike love for one another.

Generosity Conquers Selfishness

The great danger for family life, in the midst of any society whose idols are pleasure, comfort, and independence, lies in the fact that people close their hearts and become selfish.

—Saint John Paul II

You will be enriched in every way for great generosity.

—2 Corinthians 9:11

The goal of this chapter is to help couples understand how selfishness can be overcome by growth in generosity. This virtue protects marriages from the powerful force of selfishness, which John Paul II described as the greatest danger to love. When the origins of selfishness are uncovered, and the damage caused by it are revealed, the process of conquering this leading cause of marital conflict and divorce can begin through the cultivation of generosity.

The good news for couples is that generosity increases marital happiness. A 2013 national study found a correlation between high marital quality and high levels of generosity. The study of 1,365 couples found that generosity, as defined by small acts of kindness, displays of respect and

John Paul II, homily on Capital Mall, Washington, D.C. (October 7, 1979), no. 4.

affection, and a willingness to forgive faults and failings, was positively associated with marital satisfaction and negatively associated with marital conflict and perceived likelihood of divorce.[1]

Ken and Sandra

Sandra smiled broadly as she entered my office, but her puffy red eyes told the real story. Within a few minutes, the reason for her visit came pouring out. "I don't know what's wrong," she said, fiddling with her fingers. "I really love Ken, but something's missing in our relationship." She went on to explain that the first years of their marriage were everything she had dreamed of. Ken was loving and attentive, and after their first son was born, he was a hands-on dad.

As the next child came along, however, Ken began to spend less time at home and more time away doing activities that he enjoyed, such as jogging, fishing, golfing, and sitting in front of screens and not communicating. "I try to tell him that I need his help with the kids and to protect me from feeling lonely," Sandra said, her eyes welling up with tears. "I just can't do it all myself. But every time I try to talk to him, he just tells me that I'm being selfish. He points out how hard he works to support us—and he does. But is it selfish for me to want him to spend time with us instead of spending so much time at work and watching sports, and playing golf all weekend with his buddies?" The tears began to stream down her cheeks. "Sometimes I

[1] Jeffrey Dew and W. Bradford Wilcox, "Generosity and the Maintenance of Marital Quality", *Journal of Marriage and Family* 15 (September 3, 2013): 1218–28, https://doi.org/10.1111/jomf.12066.

feel like I'm less important to him than his big-screen TV and the Internet."

Ken attended the next session and appeared to be a man of integrity and faith who seemed puzzled by his wife's complaints. He related, "I work hard for my wife and children; I don't see what I'm doing wrong. I'm just trying to relax in the same ways that my dad did." He added that he didn't realize how much Sandra felt hurt and unsupported because of the amount of time he spent away from her and the children.

It is a story I have heard many times. Sandra's pain was not just a product of her imagination. Without realizing it, Ken had given in to the powerful pull of selfishness. Gradually he turned in on himself and away from his wife and children. He disguised his selfishness as his need for relaxation to compensate for the demands of his job. He felt that his hard work had earned him the leisure he was enjoying. But the fact was that selfishness had changed Ken. He was thinking more about himself and less about his wife and children and was placing his desires and needs ahead of theirs. Believing that Ken deserved his recreation time, Sandra had unwittingly enabled his behavior.

Ken was very responsive to Sandra's concern and expressed a strong desire to make changes to protect her from the sadness she was experiencing because of his inattentiveness. He said, "Sandra, I love you and never want to hurt you. I thought marriage worked by the husband doing what he wanted after work, as my dad did, and the wife supporting this behavior, as my mother did." Neither he nor Sandra had been taught that the true nature of marriage is complete self-giving love modeled after the relationship of Christ and his Bride, the Church.

Although unaware of his selfishness, Ken had been harboring anger toward Sandra for what he saw as hers. He thought that she had become too preoccupied with material possessions and her physical appearance. At times, he felt appreciated by Sandra, but at other times he felt used by her. Above all, he was deeply hurt that she was not open to his desire to have a third child. He believed that Sandra's opposition to another child was motivated by her selfish unwillingness to take on the sacrificial giving associated with mothering a larger family.

As we reviewed the symptoms of selfishness, this marital conflict was more fully uncovered and brought into the light. Ken and Sandra slowly and painfully recognized that they both had given in to selfishness and had become increasingly self-centered. They both had been thinking more often in terms of "me" and less often in terms of "we". Sandra admitted that she hadn't realized how important it was to Ken to have another child, and Ken recognized that he had been repeating his father's selfish behaviors.

Both Sandra and Ken were aware of the deep goodness in each other and were sorry for the mistakes they had made. After they understood their situation better, they were highly motivated to rid their marriage of selfishness by growing in the virtue of generosity. They agreed to make a commitment to work toward being more generous and self-giving to each other. During this process, they came to a greater recognition that sacrificial self-giving was essential to their marital happiness.

Selfishness: Its Manifestations

Selfishness is the major enemy of married love and of life-long commitment in marriage. It also undermines a person's ability to remain in the priesthood and the religious life. Saint John Paul II warned about selfishness in his Letter to Families *Gratissimam sane*:

> The dangers faced by love are also dangers for the civiliza-
> tion of love.... Here one thinks first of *selfishness*, not only
> the selfishness of individuals, but also of couples or, even
> more broadly, of social selfishness.... Selfishness in all its
> forms is directly and radically opposed to the civilization
> of love.[2]

This description is psychologically accurate. Selfishness seriously damages and can even destroy a marriage.

Selfishness often grows so quietly that couples do not recognize that it is a source of their conflicts. Behaviors that indicate selfishness include attempting to control others, harboring excessive anger, having an intense sense of superiority, and manifesting strong levels of aggressiveness when challenged.[3]

The diagnostic manual for psychiatrists has identified a number of other symptoms in those people for whom selfishness is a serious personality disorder. These include exploitation of others, manipulativeness, deceitfulness, callousness, irresponsibility, impulsivity, emotional lability, risk taking, lack of empathy, and incapacity for intimate relationships.[4]

Selfishness Checklist

Spouses commonly fail to recognize and to address selfish thinking and behavior in their marriage primarily because

[2] John Paul II, Letter to Families *Gratissimam sane* (February 2, 1994), no. 14.

[3] Christopher Peterson and Martin Seligman, *Character Strengths and Virtues: A Handbook and Classification* (Washington, D.C.: American Psychological Association, 2004), 467.

[4] American Psychiatric Association, *Diagnostic and Statistical Manual of Psychiatric Disorders*, 4th ed. (Washington, D.C.: American Psychiatric Association, 2013), 53.

they deny their selfishness or believe their behavior is normal. Another reason is the fear of a spouse's anger if this weakness is uncovered and addressed. Ken and Sandra worked to identify the manifestations of selfishness in themselves and each other with this checklist:

- Withdrawal into oneself with poor communication
- Lack of giving to romantic love
- Treatment of one's spouse as a sexual object
- Lack of respect toward one's spouse
- Overly controlling behaviors
- Overreactions in anger
- Failure to treat one's spouse as one's best friend
- Failure to wish the best for one's spouse
- Weakness in giving praise
- Excessive anger when everything does not go as expected
- Insistence on having one's own way
- Strong desire to do what one's feelings urge one to do
- Focus on one's own happiness and not on the happiness of the other
- Tendency to avoid responsibility in some major area of life
- An exaggerated sense of self-importance
- Loss of kindness and thoughtfulness
- Immature and excessive comfort-seeking behaviors
- Obsession with working out, physical appearance, and possessions
- Excessive self-indulgence
- Blind ambition for success
- Focus on the impression one produces rather than on one's work
- Loss of faith
- Lack of motivation to resolve marital conflicts

- Lack of openness to God's will regarding the size of one's family
- Lack of a sense of oneness and shared mission with one's spouse
- Failure to correct one's children and one's spouse
- Resentment of the need for self-denial and sacrificial giving
- Use of pornography
- Use of contraceptives
- Entitlement mentality

Ken and Sandra were surprised by how many symptoms of selfishness were present in their lives. They came to recognize that spending excessive time in seemingly innocent pursuits had turned them in on themselves, which interfered with the sensitive self-giving that is essential to sustaining the marital friendship. Ken said, "There has been a sneak attack on our marriage, and no one warned us about the dangers of selfishness."

The good news is that no matter how many of the above behaviors are present in a marriage, there is no need to be discouraged. Through the hard work of growing in self-knowledge and the virtue of generosity, selfishness can be overcome.

The Harm from Selfishness

Having been created male and female in the image of the trinitarian God, people are hardwired to give themselves to others. Self-giving is essential to human fulfillment and happiness. For most people, the call to self-giving is realized in marriage, as described by John Paul II in his apostolic letter *On the Dignity and Vocation of Women*:

The fact that man "created as man and woman" is the image of God means not only that each of them individually is like God, as a rational and free being. It also means that man and woman, created as a "unity of the two" in their common humanity, are called to live in a communion of love, and in this way to mirror in the world the communion of love that is in God, through which the Three Persons love each other in the intimate mystery of the one divine life.[5]

Some might think that John Paul II's idea of marriage is a Christian ideal that is irrelevant or out of reach for most people. But John Paul II took his cues not only from his faith but also from the lived experiences of real people. He saw that people are happiest when they give themselves in love to others and that selfishness does great harm to individuals, families, and communities.

The Harm to Spouses

The failure of spouses to give themselves completely to each other can result in sadness, anger, mistrust, anxiety, loss of confidence, and various types of compulsive behaviors. A person's selfishness can also contribute to the development of depression in his spouse, because of the loneliness the neglected spouse experiences.

Unless properly addressed, the conflicts caused by selfishness can ultimately lead to separation and divorce, "for love can endure only as a unity in which the mature 'we' finds clear expression, and will not endure as a combination of two egoisms".[6] According to the *Catechism*

---

[5] John Paul II, apostolic letter *Mulieris dignitatum* (On the Dignity and Vocation of Women) (August 15, 1988), no. 7.

[6] Karol Wojtyla, *Love and Responsibility* (San Francisco: Ignatius Press, 1993), 88.

of the Catholic Church (*CCC*), divorce is harmful, even immoral, because it "introduces disorder into the family and into society. This disorder brings grave harm to the deserted spouse, to children traumatized by the separation of their parents and often torn between them, and because of its contagious effect which makes it truly a plague on society" (2385).

The Harm to Children

Selfishness in one or both spouses, even if it does not result in divorce, harms their children in numerous ways. First, selfishness prevents parents from giving their children the love they need in order to develop into secure, well-adjusted adults. The absence of psychologically and spiritually healthy self-giving to children can cause them to develop sadness with secondary anger and defiant behaviors. Such children experience difficulty with trust and can suffer from subsequent anxiety disorders and the fear of parental divorce.

Selfishness can lead to permissive parenting, in which the overindulgence of children interferes with their healthy personality development. Children who are not corrected early and often about selfishness have great difficulty with controlling their anger and other strong emotions, and they do not develop an adequate sensitivity to others.

Marriages are also harmed by the failure to correct selfishness in children. When a selfish child verbally abuses his mother in an outburst of anger, and his father refuses to correct him, his mother might lose the ability to respect her husband because of his failure to protect her. Such a loss of trust can further undermine a marriage already weakened by selfishness.

As I have seen in my clinical practice, permissive parenting has been increasing, and there has been an explosion of selfishness and secondary controlling, disrespectful, and angry behaviors in children toward their parents, siblings, teachers, and peers. Self-absorbed children rarely apologize for their harmful behaviors; in fact, they often blame their parents for them.

The early and regular correction of selfishness in children is a manifestation of what John Paul II has described as responsible fatherhood and motherhood. Educating youth on the dangers of selfishness to them and to the family is essential for protecting them from narcissism, which can lead youth to think that they are entitled to have and to do whatever they desire and to overreact in anger if those desires are not fulfilled. Catholic parents need to be united in understanding the importance of correcting this leading personality weakness for the psychological health of their children and for the protection of their marriage and family life.

The Harm to the Church

Selfishness has damaged not only Catholic marriages but also vocations to the priesthood and the religious life. Some forty years ago, the Catholic Church in the United States had almost 170,000 nuns, more than 50,000 priests, more than 10,000 brothers, and more than 40,000 seminarians. In 2000, there were 81,000 nuns, 46,000 priests (with 8,000 listed as retired, sick, or absent), fewer than 6,000 brothers, and 4,500 seminarians. There can be little doubt that the selfishness encouraged by our materialist, individualist culture has played a role in this decline.[7] It has also played a role in the sexual abuse crisis in the Church, for the inability

[7] Dermott J. Mullan, "The Catholic Hiroshima", *New Oxford Review* (September 2001), https://www.newoxfordreview.org/documents/the-catholic-hiroshima/.

to control sexual impulses in order not to harm a child is a manifestation of extreme self-absorption.[8]

Origins of Selfishness

Many spouses, even those who entered the married state as thoughtful, loving, and sensitive, can be drawn away from self-giving by the powerful pull of selfishness. The following are major causes of this enemy of love.

Culture of Selfishness

The siren song of selfishness exerts a powerful influence in our culture. Our cravings for pleasure and comfort are constantly being aroused by entertainment and advertisements that entice us to seek the fulfillment of our every desire. Selfishness pulls us away from God, making it harder for us to deny ourselves in order to love our spouses and our children. If we fail to fight daily against selfishness, we unconsciously turn in on ourselves, closing off our hearts to others. Our ability to cherish and to treat our spouses with respect weakens, and our tendency to dominate others to achieve our own ends grows stronger.

False Understanding of Freedom

A mistaken notion of freedom has strongly influenced the spread of selfishness in marriages. Many people assume that the purpose of freedom is to do as one pleases, that limits on one's freedom are to be avoided. But as Bishop Karol Wojtyla (later Pope John Paul II) explained, the purpose of

---

[8] Richard Fitzgibbons and Dale O'Leary, "Sexual Abuse of Minors by Catholic Clergy", *Linacre Quarterly* 78, no. 3 (August 1, 2011): 252–73.

freedom is to choose to make a gift of oneself to another. When a person chooses to marry, he voluntarily puts a limit on his freedom in order to give himself completely to his spouse. "Limitation of one's freedom might seem to be something negative and unpleasant, but love makes it a positive, joyful and creative thing. *Freedom exists for the sake of love.*"[9] With this true understanding of freedom in the service of love, couples can choose to rise above self-seeking and to commit themselves more fully to their spouses and their children.

Original Sin

Pope Benedict XVI spoke of a "poisonous root of selfishness which does evil to oneself and to others".[10] He was referring to the damage caused by Original Sin, the first sin committed by mankind, when our first parents chose their vanity and pride over obedience to their Creator. The tendency toward selfishness that we are born with can be observed by any parent of a toddler who shouts "Mine!" when an object he desires is held by someone else. It is only at three and a half to four years of age, after much patient correction and good example by parents, that children are finally willing to take turns and to share with others. Likewise, it is only through constant effort, aided by grace, that adults can continue to overcome their selfish tendencies.

Lack of Character Development

The significant dangers of self-love used to be communicated in families, churches, and schools in order to

[9] Wojtyla, *Love and Responsibility*, p.135. Emphasis in the original.
[10] Pope Benedict XVI, address on the Solemnity of the Immaculate Conception (December 8, 2012).

encourage the development of good character. Catholics were taught that the dangers of self-love could even lead to hatred of God, as Saint Augustine warned. But decades of pop psychology promoting inflated self-esteem, permissive parenting, and moral relativism have made a "me first" attitude commonplace. As a result, exaggerated self-love leads many husbands and wives to be obsessed with their own desires and pursuits, to the detriment of those whom they vowed to cherish. For many, the moral responsibility to seek the good of one's spouse and children has been replaced by an obsession with taking care of oneself.

Contraceptive Mentality

Before the 1960s, Catholics accepted the Church's moral teaching as the standard of right and wrong. They sinned, of course, but they rarely claimed to be Catholic if they rejected fundamental teachings of the Church. With the advent of the sexual revolution, however, fueled by the birth control pill's promise of child-free sex, many Catholics expected the Church to change her teaching. When Pope Paul VI, in his 1968 encyclical *Humanae vitae* (On the Regulation of Birth), reaffirmed the constant teaching of the Church on the immorality of using contraception, many Catholics rebelled. They asserted that their consciences condoned the use of contraceptives in their particular circumstances.

While some clergy and religious supported the use of contraception based on a flawed understanding of human biology and anthropology, even faithful clergy, including bishops, lacked the knowledge or the courage to articulate the Church's teaching on contraception effectively. Their silence resulted in widespread acceptance and use of contraceptives among Catholics, which was encouraged by the doctors and the pharmaceutical companies that profit from them.

Many Catholics soon conformed to the secular model of the two-child family. Other factors besides the availability of contraception contributed to this. The rising costs of education, housing, and health care convinced many Catholic couples that they could not afford to raise the large families their parents did. Feminists and environmentalists tried to persuade them that it would be immoral to try. They lost hope that their future children would be precious assets to their family, the Church, and the world. As Catholics put more faith in their material prosperity than in God, they lost trust in divine providence, and they consequently suffered a loss of generosity and an openness to life. Selfishness increased, and so did divorce.

Pope John Paul II tried to reverse these trends by boldly defending the Church's teaching about marriage and by demonstrating the truth that contraception damages marital love. He explained that contraception separates the sexual act from its two purposes: the total union of the spouses and the procreation of new life.

> When couples, by means of recourse to contraception, separate these two meanings that God the Creator has inscribed in the being of man and woman and in the dynamism of their sexual communion, they act as "arbiters" of the divine plan and they "manipulate" and degrade human sexuality—and with it themselves and their married partner—by altering its value of "total" self-giving. Thus the innate language that expresses the total reciprocal self-giving of husband and wife is overlaid, through contraception, by an objectively contradictory language, namely, that of not giving oneself totally to the other. This leads not only to a positive refusal to be open to life but

also to a falsification of the inner truth of conjugal love, which is called upon to give itself in personal totality.[11]

The pope spoke and wrote at great length on this subject. On one occasion, he said, "Contraception is to be judged so profoundly unlawful as never to be, for any reason, justified. To think or to say the contrary is equal to maintaining that in human life, situations may arise in which it is lawful not to recognize God as God."[12]

Throughout history, marriage has been understood to be the only institution that unites a man and a woman with each other and with any children who come into being from their sexual union. Fertility was considered a blessing, and children the "supreme gift of marriage", its "crowning glory".[13] Contraception radically changed the understanding not only of human sexuality but of fertility itself. Contraceptive or sterile recreational sex became the norm, and fertility came to be treated as something to be controlled by hormonal drugs, invasive devices, or surgery.

Once the relationships between sex and marriage and children were severed by contraception, alternatives to traditional marriage between one man and one woman exploded, and so did reproductive technologies. Marriage ceased to be a prerequisite for engaging in sexual activity or for having children. Marriage became merely a living arrangement that includes sexual access between any two people who love each other enough to commit to staying

---

[11] John Paul II, Apostolic Exhortation on the Role of the Christian Family in the Modern World *Familiaris consortio* (November 22, 1981), no. 32.

[12] John Paul II, Address to Priests Taking Part in a Study Seminar on Responsible Procreation (Rome, September 17, 1983).

[13] *CCC* 1652, quoting *GS* 50 § 1; cf. Gen 2:18; Mt 19:4; Gen 1:28 and *GS* 48 § 1; 50.

together as long as both are happy. Anyone can obtain a child or avoid having a child, according to preference.

Because of the contraceptive mentality, a significant number of Catholic youth are growing up with only one sibling or none, which can deny them the opportunity to grow in the virtues that foster healthy personality development, such as self-denial and generosity. In addition, many youths are unconsciously modeling themselves after parents who embraced both contraception and materialism, and perhaps even divorced. The ability of these young Catholics to give themselves later in marriage and to trust in God's providence for their lives is being harmed, and the result is a massive retreat from marriage and family life.[14]

Generosity, the Antidote to Selfishness

When Ken and Sandra compared their behaviors with the selfishness checklist in this chapter and reflected on the harm they had caused each other, their marriage, and their children, they became highly motivated to make changes for the better. "If I were bitten by a venomous snake, I would need to apply an immediate antidote so that the poison wouldn't spread and kill me," Ken said. "The same is true for selfishness." He and Sandra were pleased to learn that the most effective antidote to selfishness is generosity, and that it was within their power, with the help of grace, to acquire this virtue.

First, Ken took the initiative to ask Sandra for forgiveness for all the ways his selfish behaviors had hurt her over the course of their marriage. Sandra tearfully

---

[14] Center for Applied Research in the Apostolate, *Frequently Requested Church Statistics*, https://cara.georgetown.edu/frequently-requested-church-statistics/.

responded that she would try to forgive, but she admitted that it would be difficult for her. She then asked Ken for forgiveness for wanting to limit their family to two children. Ken and Sandra then requested forgiveness from their children for any hurts they had caused them by their unrecognized selfishness.

Next, Ken and Sandra took to heart Saint Augustine's advice: "The first labor is, that you should be displeasing to yourself, that sins you should battle out, that you should be changed into something better."[15] Ken vowed to change his attitude and behaviors: he would no longer be self-focused and instead would try to demonstrate his love for his wife by generous, self-sacrificing acts. Sandra, too, made a commitment to change her thinking and behaviors.

The habit of generosity helps people to move beyond their petty concerns so that they can give themselves more fully and cheerfully to others, particularly to their spouses. Generosity helps spouses to expand the focus of their thoughts and actions beyond their narrow desires, to encompass the greater "we" of marriage and family life. Growth in this habit awakens in spouses a desire to be more giving and to look for ways in which they can bring more love into their families. Generosity also helps with the following:

- Understanding that love is demonstrated by deeds more than words
- Desiring the best for one's spouse

[15] Augustine, *Exposition on Psalm 60*, Nicene and Post-Nicene Fathers 1, vol. 8, trans. J. E. Tweed, ed. Philip Schaff (Buffalo, N.Y.: Christian Literature, 1888), no. 5; revised and edited for New Advent by Kevin Knight, http://www.newadvent.org/fathers/1801060.htm.

- Viewing one's spouse as a gift from God and a treasure to be cherished
- Letting go of the tendency to be overly independent
- Being willing to rely on one's spouse
- Being willing to share in decision-making
- Recognizing the need to establish balance and priorities
- Being more concerned about the needs of one's spouse than about one's own needs
- Preferring that attention and conversation not be focused on oneself
- Believing that one's spouse is second only to God in one's heart and mind
- Committing to model the good traits of one's parents but not their selfishness
- Trusting that God's grace and support can help one to overcome harmful behaviors.

The habit of generosity is manifested in some of these ways:

- Expressing love and affection through both words and deeds
- Offering far more positive than negative comments to one's spouse
- Setting aside time daily to talk together
- Having dinner together as often as possible
- Opening the home more often to family and friends
- Giving cheerfully
- Correcting each other and the children charitably when selfishness is observed
- Giving more generously to charities
- Praying together
- Learning about Natural Family Planning and stopping the use of contraception

Putting It into Practice

Ken and Sandra developed personal checklists of ways to grow in generosity based on the lists above. Each week they reviewed their lists together and offered one another feedback and encouragement. As they made progress in becoming more generous with each other, their children, and others, they experienced a deeper sense of fulfillment. Ken could look back at where they had started and see that in the past he had given much more of himself to his work and sports than to his wife and his children. He explained, "Now I see that I had become imprisoned in my own selfishness. Now my heart is more open. I feel more fulfilled and happier by placing Sandra and the children before myself."

Selfishness is so ingrained in the human condition that, naturally, there were times when Ken and Sandra stumbled. Growth in virtues requires hard work and perseverance. Spouses need to adopt a sporting spirit in this long-term effort so that after a "relapse" an apology is graciously offered and accepted, and both recommit to the struggle. Ken admitted, "One of my greatest challenges is to stop being as independent and self-preoccupied as my father had been. It's scary how powerful this bad habit has been in my life."

Sandra struggled initially to understand how she had hurt Ken by not wanting to have more children. From her perspective, "he didn't seem that intense or strong about this issue. He only mentioned it several times." But as she grew in her understanding of Church teaching on marriage—through reading some of John Paul II's writings—her heart expanded. She became more aware of the beauty of her vocational calling to be open to God's gift of children, consistent with the Church's teaching on responsible parenthood. She was particularly moved by this passage from John Paul II's *Letter to Women*:

> Thank you, *women who are mothers!* You have sheltered human beings within yourselves in a unique experience of joy and travail. This experience makes you become God's own smile upon the newborn child, the one who guides your child's first steps, who helps it to grow, and who is the anchor as the child makes its way along the journey of life.[16]

Sandra asked Ken to forgive her for insisting that they use contraceptives—despite what the Church teaches—and for having refused to consider his desire, and their calling, to be open to the gift of life. After Sandra made an effort to understand the Catholic vision of marriage and family life, she and Ken agreed to stop using contraceptives. They took a brief course in Natural Family Planning, which taught them how to read the signs of Sandra's fertility. They found this knowledge to be empowering, as they took responsibility together for timing their sexual relations and planning the size of their family.

Correction and Forgiveness

Ken and Sandra experienced at times the common difficulty of failing to offer charitable correction of selfish behavior. Their own parents had not given gentle, loving correction to each other, so this practice was unknown to them. As they were highly motivated to rid their marriage of selfishness, however, they prayed for the grace to correct

[16] John Paul II, *Letter to Women* (June 29, 1995), no. 2. Emphasis in the original.

each other properly, as counseled by Saint Paul: "Teach and admonish one another in all wisdom" (Col 3:16).

Ken and Sandra wrote a list of the areas in which they needed to grow in self-denial. As with their lists of generous thoughts and actions, they reviewed these resolutions together weekly and offered each other gentle corrections for relapses into bad habits. Their corrections were followed by asking and giving forgiveness, along with words of encouragement to persevere in their mutual quest for greater generosity and self-denial. Forgiveness helped Ken and Sandra repeatedly during their healing journey. When one of them slipped back into old selfish habits, the other's first response was to think about forgiving before offering a correction.

The couple soon realized that they also needed to correct the selfishness in their two children. It was painful for them to recognize that their selfishness had imprinted itself on their children, who resented having to contribute to the good of the family, even in doing the smallest chores. Their eyes were opened to the truth that both of their children spent far too much time isolating themselves from others with their computers, video games, smartphones, and televisions.

As Sandra and Ken became more generous in giving themselves, they experienced greater happiness and less preoccupation with their own needs. They discovered that their previous individual pursuits of ease and pleasure had brought them loneliness, sadness, isolation, lack of fulfillment, anxiety, and an insatiable need for more possessions and diversions. They recognized that their marital friendship and their relationships with their children had suffered because everyone in the family had spent most evenings and weekends apart from each other. Together, they committed to change their weekend schedule so that they could keep Sundays for the Lord and for their family. Spending time together took priority over all the activities they used to pursue on their own, and their family grew closer together in greater mutual love and respect.

The Benefits of Faith

Ken and Sandra found tremendous support for their growth in generosity through the practice of their Catholic faith. The Catholic Church considers marriage a sacrament, a channel of God's grace, and a powerful help in the struggle against selfishness: "Marriage helps to overcome self-absorption, egoism, pursuit of one's own pleasure, and to open oneself to the other, to mutual aid and to self-giving" (*CCC* 1609).

As both spouses grew in their commitment to serve each other and their children, they found that their hearts expanded toward other family members and those in need. They began tithing to their parish and contributing to the parish food bank and other charities. They found in the Church the encouragement and the opportunities they needed to practice generosity both inside and outside their immediate family.

Faith assists many spouses in winning the battle against selfishness—the powerful enemy of marital love. Numerous studies have confirmed the beneficial effects of faith on marital happiness, as well as on psychological health. Catholic couples report being helped by daily prayer, the practice of self-denial and temperance, a daily examination of conscience, and the regular reception of the Sacraments of Reconciliation and the Eucharist. Others tell of the benefits from Eucharistic adoration, devotion to the Sacred Heart, and the Rosary.

Prayer plays a prominent role, for it increases the virtue of faith, which helps to diminish many of the worries and pressures from which spouses can seek escape through selfish behaviors. The main reason prayer is so beneficial is that it takes the eyes off self and directs them to God. As Father Romano Guardini observed, "Keeping our eyes upon ourself makes us crooked."[17] Setting our eyes on God fills us with love for him and the desire to serve him by loving others.

The hard work done by Ken and Sandra to grow in the virtue of generosity bore fruit in greater marital and personal happiness and in the discovery that they were expecting a baby. Greater self-giving brought each of them greater fulfillment. Their experience confirmed the truth expressed in this statement by the Second Vatican Council and often repeated by John Paul II: "Man ... cannot fully find himself except through a sincere gift of himself."[18] Ken and Sandra found their true selves and marital happiness by conquering selfishness.

[17] Romano Guardini, *Learning the Virtues That Lead You to God* (Manchester, N.H.: Sophia Institute Press, 1998), 154.

[18] Vatican Council II, Pastoral Constitution on the Church in the Modern World *Gaudium et spes* (December 7, 1965), no. 24.

3

Respect Overcomes the Urge to Control

Inspired and sustained by the new commandment of love, the Christian family welcomes, respects and serves every human being, considering each one in his or her dignity as a person and as a child of God.

—Saint John Paul II

Outdo one another in showing honor.

—Romans 12:10

The goal of this chapter is to help spouses understand the importance of the habit of respect in addressing the common problem of controlling behavior. The causes of controlling behavior and the harm it does to spouses and children are identified. The habit of respect is described, as is its application to feeling, thinking, acting, and communicating. In addition, the benefits of forgiveness for the controlling spouse and the victim spouse and the role of faith in overcoming controlling tendencies are presented.

John Paul II, Apostolic Exhortation on the Role of the Christian Family in the Modern World *Familiaris consortio* (November 22, 1981), no. 64.

Shawn and Brittany

"Our marriage was great in the beginning," Shawn said in our first session. He had come for treatment because he had been experiencing increasing anxiety. "But lately, it seems like Brittany is upset all the time. I think it's because I'm so insecure and nervous. I love her, but I feel I want to avoid her so that I have some peace in my life."

As we talked, Shawn came to understand that he was blaming himself exclusively for the tensions in his marriage, but the problem did not rest on his shoulders alone. Brittany tended to become irritable when she did not feel that she was in control. The more she tried to control Shawn, the more insecure and anxious he became. Their marriage was on a downward spiral that resulted in Shawn's developing intense anxiety and anger, a loss of trust in his wife, and a desire to distance himself from her.

Controlling behavior is a common cause of tension and unhappiness in married life. I have found that only selfishness and excessive anger cause more harm to marriage. Spouses who give in to this personality weakness are often unaware that they are doing so. Controlling behaviors occur when one spouse sincerely believes that he knows better than the other spouse about what's best for the family. Controlling spouses are often unaware of this personality weakness that drives their behaviors and of the harm they inflict upon the person they most love.

Some controlling spouses, however, know exactly what they are doing, and they cleverly and skillfully mask their desire to dominate. Such a person can assume the role of victim, for example, in order to dominate others. With such duplicity, marital conflict can go undetected for years or even decades, and uncovering it can be challenging.

It was only after ten years of married life that Shawn identified his wife's controlling behavior. His denial of the harm it was doing to their relationship weakened over time and then finally collapsed under the weight of emotional pain and stress caused by her disrespectful treatment. When Shawn finally explained to Brittany how her behavior had been hurting him and requested that she treat him with more respect, she expressed a desire to change.

Brittany was able to identify that her need to control was the result of childhood trauma caused by her father's alcoholism and anger. Unconsciously, she felt that if she were in control, she could prevent the turmoil of her childhood from recurring in her marriage and family life. Brittany never meant to hurt Shawn, and she apologized for her many years of disrespectful treatment.

The Causes of Controlling Behaviors

The most common cause of controlling behaviors in marriage is a lack of trust resulting from family-of-origin hurts. The unconscious fear of being hurt again causes anxiety, which results in attempts at controlling others through disrespectful, manipulative behaviors. These behaviors are often modeled after a controlling parent. A common component of these behaviors is anger at the parent that is misdirected at one's spouse. The innocent spouse's wound from being treated disrespectfully is then compounded by the pain inflicted by the controlling spouse's anger.

In my clinical experience of over forty years, I have found that the most common unresolved childhood conflicts in wives come from having a father who was selfish, alcoholic, unfaithful, controlling, or excessively angry. Experiences with such a father weaken self-confidence and the ability to trust. In husbands, the unresolved childhood hurts often involve a weakness in male confidence from a lack of affirmation in the father-son relationship. For both husbands and wives, the effort to feel superior to one's spouse through domination is an unconscious attempt to escape from the pain of insecurity and to boost one's self-esteem. In such cases, modeling after a controlling mother is not uncommon.

Today, the divorce of one's parents is one of the leading family-of-origin conflicts that cause childhood fears and damage the ability to feel safe in loving relationships. The damage to trust in the children of divorce regularly leads to their being either controlling or fearful of commitment.

Here is a list of the most common causes of controlling behaviors in marriage:

- Lack of secure attachment to one's mother
- Lack of a close father relationship
- Selfishness
- Modeling after a controlling parent
- Lack of appropriate responsibility in one's spouse
- Substance abuse in a parent
- Parental enabling of controlling, selfish behaviors
- Significant hurts in previous relationships
- Failure to balance a strong personality with the virtue of gentleness
- Loss of trust from serious hurts in family or work relationships
- Parental infidelity
- Severe family problems, deaths, or tragedies
- Mistrustful thinking about men or women
- Guilt over inappropriate behaviors
- Lack of faith

If spouses are able to identify causes of controlling behaviors in themselves or in their husbands or wives, they should not be discouraged! Even if one has deep emotional conflicts arising from childhood hurts, they can be resolved. In the healing journey, faith helps many spouses come to believe that the loving God, who knows that his sons and daughters were wounded in childhood, will offer a way to heal such hurts so that they can feel safe in his providence.

Although Brittany had attended Adult Children of Alcoholics meetings and thought she had resolved her anger with her father by forgiving him, she eventually understood that her critical and controlling behaviors pointed to a father wound that had not completely healed. Shawn was also able to recognize that he had unresolved issues with his father due to his father's having been emotionally insensitive to his mother. Because no one comes from a perfect family, the identification of weaknesses in each spouse's family of origin helps in marital healing. One spouse rarely causes all the marital conflicts.

Uncovering Controlling Conflicts

The following checklists can help couples to uncover controlling behaviors in their marriages. Many controlling behaviors are not deliberately chosen but are instead activated and employed because of an unconscious fear of being hurt. The tendency to control can be seen in the following behaviors:

- Disrespectful speech
- Excessive anger or criticism
- Inability to listen
- Constant texting or calling
- Making all decisions about family activities and friendships

- Interference in the other spouse's parenting without cause
- Emotional distance and difficulty in giving and receiving affection
- Difficulty in giving praise

Another sign of the tendency to dominate is the attempt to isolate one's spouse from friends and relatives. Under pressure from controlling spouses, husbands or wives might feel a lack of freedom to appreciate and to express their unique personalities and then withdraw from relationships and activities outside the family.

Controlling spouses employ various strategies to get their way. Among these are the following:

- Blaming the other spouse for conflicts in the marriage
- Using anger to intimidate one's spouse
- Using criticism to undermine the confidence of one's spouse
- Acting as a victim or feigning illness
- Acting hysterical
- Restricting access to family finances
- Acting in manipulative ways
- Using religion to make a spouse feel guilty or insecure
- Making one's spouse feel overly dependent
- Making unreasonable demands
- Making threats of ending the marriage

Controlling Spouses and the Alienation of Children

When a person shows disrespect to a spouse in front of their children, it can undermine that spouse's relationship with them and lead the children to model the disrespectful behavior of the controlling spouse. The message that is given to children in such marriages is that they need not take seriously or listen to the disrespected parent.

Some controlling spouses are so impaired by their compulsion to dominate others that they falsely come to view their husbands or wives as being dangerous to their children. Often, this is a projection onto their husbands or wives of a conflict these spouses had with one of their parents, most often the father, who was angry, demanding, abusive, addicted, or disloyal.

These spouses set out to undermine the trust of the children in their father or mother and, sadly, may accomplish their goal. Husbands may be falsely accused of being autistic when, in fact, they are quiet men whose trust has been damaged by a controlling wife who could not trust her father. Wives who believe in the Church's teaching on sexual morality may be called religious fanatics by husbands who had controlling or permissive mothers who spoiled them.

Justice requires that behaviors aimed at alienating children from their parents be uncovered and addressed in the family in order to protect essential, secure relationships between child and parent. Children need stable relationships with both parents, contrary to the claim made by controlling spouses that one loving parent is enough.

The Sudden Emergence of Controlling Behaviors

Many people with deep-seated controlling compulsions work hard to keep this personality weakness under wraps while dating or engaged in order to win the heart of their loved ones. As the Italian saying goes, they try to make *la bella figura*, the best impression (literally, "the beautiful figure"). A warning sign prior to marriage is the pressure to cohabit, which can be a manifestation of a desire to dominate early in the relationship.

However well disguised the urge to control might be prior to marriage, it will typically emerge soon after the wedding, perhaps even during the honeymoon, at times causing the victim spouse to wonder, "Who is this person I married? How could I have been so blind?"

The conflict can also erupt after the birth of the first child, when it is essential to trust one's spouse in the new role of parent. If one of the spouses had difficulty in trusting a parent, then unrecognized and unresolved anxiety and anger may undermine the ability to have confidence in the other spouse as a parent. Spouses attempting to cope with this pain begin engaging in controlling behaviors, such as angry overreactions. The psychological dynamic here is that, as trust drops, anger rises. All of this occurs on an unconscious level, and attempts to uncover the causes of angry outbursts are often met with vigorous denials.

After the birth of her first child, Brittany became more critical and mistrustful of Shawn. He was baffled by the change and, initially, thought she might be experiencing a postpartum emotional state. He later realized that the conflict was much deeper, and the growing stress in their communication and the weakening of their marital friendship saddened and confused him.

Controlling behaviors can emerge for the first time as a result of other stresses that weaken trust. These include having a controlling and critical boss, the loss of a job, financial setbacks, or the serious illness of a child. Some spouses become controlling under the influence of selfishness in the surrounding culture or in friends who have embraced a "me first" view of marriage and attempt to meet their needs through manipulative behavior.

The Harm from Controlling Behaviors

Most controlling spouses fail to grasp the extent of the pain they inflict on their spouses and their children. A victim spouse may experience a loss of trust, a decrease in feelings of love, avoidance, anxiety, sadness and loneliness, mistrust and defensiveness, muscular tension, insecurity, diminished sexual responsiveness, and anger. After many years of disrespectful treatment, the victim spouse may develop an emotional vulnerability to sensitive, respectful treatment by the opposite sex.

The victim spouse may react to controlling behavior with a decreased desire to communicate and an increased desire for comfort from food, alcohol, pornography, or extramarital relationships. A variety of psychosomatic disorders may develop, such as irritable bowel syndrome, chronic headaches, muscular spasms, and fibromyalgia.

Controlling spouses can also pay a high price for their personality weakness. They can often experience loneliness as a result of difficulty in maintaining healthy friendships. No one enjoys being close to a controlling person. Not infrequently, children will put up walls between themselves and a controlling parent before and after leaving the home. The controlling person's loneliness may later develop into depressive illness. Unless a decision is made to address this personality conflict, controlling behavior can lead to marital separation or even divorce.

The Harm to Children

Shawn and Brittany's three children were emotionally wounded by the criticism, tension, and anger that weakened the marital love and friendship of their parents. The heart of a child understands that everyone should be treated with respect and kindness, particularly within the family. The absence of respectful behaviors creates sadness within children, because they fail to experience the flow of love between their parents that is necessary for their happiness and psychological health. They feel that their parents are not one but rather two people who do not love each other.

Because controlling spouses are often controlling parents, as the years go by, children struggle with anger toward the domineering parent, which can be misdirected at siblings or at persons of the controlling parent's sex. The significant stress in these homes can also lead to the development of oppositional defiant disorder and anxiety disorders in children.

The children of controlling people can develop an unconscious fear that they will be treated in a similar way after they are married. This fear is a major factor that influences the retreat from marriage or the need to control later in married life. If a child's parents divorced, the fear of relationships can be even more pronounced. Judith Wallerstein, in her first major work on the children of divorce, wrote: "Anxiety about relationships was at the bedrock of their personalities, and endured even in happy marriages."[1] Fortunately, the reality of how children are harmed by controlling behaviors motivates some spouses to undertake the hard work of mastering this powerful conflict.

The Need for Respect

The controlling personality weakness is one of the most difficult psychological conflicts to overcome. The reasons

[1] Judith Wallerstein, *The Unexpected Legacy of Divorce* (New York: Hyperion, 2000), 300.

for this include the serious childhood trauma that has caused deeply rooted fears, the lifelong modeling after a controlling parent, and selfishness. Overcoming this major enemy of marital love and psychological health requires humility to admit its presence and origins, as well as hard work. The battle for freedom from the urge to control begins with a commitment to grow in greater respect for one's spouse.

Respect is an essential virtue for marriage and family life and is expressed in the marital vows: "I will love and honor you all the days of my life." Respect involves making a daily decision to identify and to love the goodness, the worth, and the dignity of one's spouse as a child of God and to treat him accordingly. Respect helps spouses to weigh their insights and experiences together by listening to each other and taking seriously each other's ideas. They are then able to overcome the bad habit of trying to force their ideas on each other. They come to see more clearly that their husbands or wives wish the best for them and would never deliberately want to hurt them.

Cultivating respect as a virtue does not mean accepting all the ideas, beliefs, or actions of the other person. Rather, it means recognizing the other person's basic human dignity, even when his ideas or values differ from ours. A general attitude of respect also assumes that each person has something to teach us if we are willing to learn.

Respect in marriage flows when the spouses deeply admire each other's goodness, abilities, qualities, and achievements. This respect contributed in no small measure to their being attracted to each other and to their decision to marry. But this respect can be harmed by the emergence of unresolved emotional conflicts. The good news is that despite the marital stress caused by these conflicts, the original respect can be rediscovered and strengthened.

Growth in Respect

Regardless of how long controlling behaviors and communication patterns have been present in a marriage, after they have been uncovered, they can be overcome by growing in the virtue of respect. I often begin the process by telling the story of the strong, proud, independent mountain climber who got into serious trouble on a challenging ascent and was holding on to a branch for dear life. He cried out for help, and a voice below responded, "Don't worry. I am here to help you."

"Who are you?" replied the climber.

"Jesus Christ, your Savior and Lord."

"Great! What should I do?"

"Let go."

After a long pause, the climber cried out again, "Is there anyone else down there?"

The moral of the story is that it is not easy to let go of something that seems to be providing security. People who have been fighting back fear by trying to control others will struggle to stop doing so. The healing process to conquer this character weakness is arduous, and many spouses consider leaving the marriage rather than persevering on the healing journey. Marital therapy itself can also be difficult because, naturally, the controlling spouse wants to control the counseling sessions. Thus, the healing process requires a daily commitment to personal growth.

Also needed is the hurt spouse's willingness to tell the offending spouse the truth about the harm his behavior has caused. The hurt spouse needs to ask for more respect. Once Shawn recognized that his anxiety was related to his fear of Brittany, he began to ask for the respect that she had showed him before they had children. He pointed out examples of her harmful actions in a kind manner, avoiding any anger, and this helped her to change her behavior.

Shawn was able to do this only after he engaged in forgiveness exercises (described in chapter 1) to diminish the anger that had built up over the years. His healing also involved forgiving his alcoholic father-in-law, who had made it so difficult for Brittany to trust her husband. Shawn's ability to forgive was helped by the knowledge that Brittany was a wonderful woman and a committed wife, who was acting out of unresolved fears and not out of selfishness or pride.

After Brittany was able to identify the mistrust in her heart, she was able to understand her desire to control. Her great love for Shawn and their children motivated her to engage in the hard work of forgiving her father and committing daily to growth in the major virtue that can master the tendency to control others—respect. Like others who have taken on this struggle, she made an effort to cultivate respect in her thinking, speaking, and acting.

Respect in Thinking

Growth in respect begins with changing the way we think about others, looking for their special attributes and being thankful for them. Shawn and Brittany found it helpful to read the *Letter to Catholic Bishops on the Collaboration of Men and Women in the Church and in the World*, issued in 2004 by the Congregation for the Doctrine of the Faith under its prefect Joseph Cardinal Ratzinger (who later became Pope Benedict XVI). Describing the unique, complementary aspects of masculinity and femininity, the document helped Shawn and Brittany to appreciate their special gifts as husband and wife and to deepen their mutual respect.

Growth in respect is also helped along by identifying the basic goodness in one's spouse and by being thankful for and loyal to that goodness. Brittany made a decision to think back to the time when she fell in love with Shawn and felt safe with him because she saw that his goodness and trustworthiness far outweighed any of his weaknesses. She used a healing journal to record ways in which he had demonstrated that he was trustworthy. She often reflected, "He was much more trustworthy than my father and does not have my father's serious conflicts. I am safe with him." This cognitive exercise decreased her negative, fearful thinking pattern and increased her trust, respect, and love for him.

Brittany also wrote a list of positive statements to correct her negative and distorted thinking about her marriage and reviewed them several times daily. They included the following:

- Shawn deserves to be treated with respect.
- Shawn wishes the best for me and is loyal.
- I want to trust and respect Shawn more each day.
- Shawn will not betray me, as my father did.
- My control weakness harms our marriage and our children.
- I want to trust God more each day.
- I am powerless over my tendency to control and want to turn it over to God.
- God is in control, not me.

Respect in Speaking

Brittany was encouraged to improve her communication style by offering five positive comments for each negative one, by listening more attentively, by avoiding interrupting, and by being more receptive to her husband's views. She also committed herself to communicate feelings of love more often and to give compliments cheerfully. As a result, she identified more clearly Shawn's many gifts as husband, father, provider, and protector. Shawn, for his part, committed himself to taking down the walls, forgiving past hurts, speaking with greater gentleness, and trusting Brittany more. Both husband and wife asked for forgiveness for painful communication experiences and set aside time every evening to communicate in a respectful, loving manner.

Respect in Acting

As Saint Josemaría Escrivá wrote, "Love means deeds and not just sweet words."[2] It is important, therefore, for spouses to demonstrate love and respect for each other by showing affection, engaging in acts of kindness, being more attentive, and denying themselves for the sake of the other. They should also protect one another from loneliness and anxiety as much as possible.

Brittany recognized that fears from her childhood tempted her to be controlling and to keep her husband at a distance. She noticed that as she worked daily on forgiving her father for past injuries and on cultivating more self-giving behaviors toward her husband, her fears decreased. Her anxiety diminished as she gave herself more fully to her husband and gave him more room to be the person he is.

Correcting a Controlling Spouse

Many spouses do not realize that they need to give gentle, clear correction to each other when necessary. They need to receive correction from each other too. Although they

[2] Josemaría Escrivá, *The Way* (New York: Scepter, 1992), no. 933.

are not aware of it, the failure to correct and to receive correction is a lack of loyalty to a marriage, because, without correction, spouses cannot grow into the people they are meant to be.

Correcting controlling people can be challenging, because, to avoid justifiable criticism, they often instill in others a fear of arousing their anger. Their response to gentle correction is often denial while pointing out the weaknesses of the person giving correction or erupting in anger in order to end communication on the topic. Mental health professionals who have the courage and the confidence to point out controlling behaviors in their clients can also be subjected to manipulative treatment. At the receiving end of angry, disrespectful comments, counselors and spouses sometimes mistakenly back down, especially when the controlling behavior is driven by selfishness or pride.

Here are the leading reasons why people can have difficulty in offering much-needed correction to controlling spouses:

- Denial of the harm caused by controlling behavior
- Fear that a spouse's angry response will cause distress in the children
- Fear of losing the spouse's love
- Lack of confidence
- Fear of separation or divorce
- Concern about the possibility of leading a materially less comfortable life
- Failure to trust the Lord with the marriage

To overcome these fears, a spouse needs to believe that correction is needed for the good of the other spouse and the marriage. When Shawn came to believe that he needed to do more to protect his marriage and his family, he worked on overcoming his insecurities and fears so that he could offer the correction his wife truly needed.

Gradually Shawn learned how to give loving correction to Brittany when she exhibited controlling behaviors. He reminded her that he loved her, that she was safe with him, and that there was no need to act in a controlling manner. He discovered that whenever Brittany was irritable and controlling, the best thing to do was to remind her that he was trustworthy and reliable. He also reminded her that there was no need to control, because the Lord was protecting them and providing for them. He was the one in control.

Correcting Controlling Parents of Spouses

A spouse's parent can be another cause of controlling behaviors. When Shawn's father would make critical comments about Brittany, Shawn would fail to defend her. As a result, Brittany's trust in her husband, which was already fragile, weakened. Since her insecurity was a cause of her need to control, criticism from Shawn's father only added to this problem in her marriage.

Shawn came to realize that he needed to show respect for his wife by standing up for her. With this new awareness, he corrected his father for the first time in his life, asking him to stop making negative comments about his wife and to start treating her with more respect. Shawn also requested that his father ask Brittany for forgiveness for the hurts of the past. His father complied because he knew that his son was right and that he would see his grandchildren less often if he did not apologize to Brittany.

Some parents think that they are entitled to interfere with their children's marriages and families. Such parents are a source of serious conflict in many marriages. They can place psychological pressure on a married child to be more loyal to his family of origin than to his spouse. This might involve the parents criticizing their son- or daughter-in-law, often for being too religious or not religious enough. Insecure husbands and wives who crave parental approval are particularly vulnerable to such criticism and will pressure their spouses to conform to the wishes of their parents. Control pressure is often more keenly felt by the wife, who is made to feel overly responsible for the happiness of extended family members.

An increasingly common cause of this difficulty is that the controlling parents chose (with the aid of contraception or sterilization) to have only one or two children themselves. With this generation of adult children now marrying later or not at all and postponing childbearing, potential grandparents may be acutely aware of the void in their lives. As a result, they may intrude in their children's marriages, attempt to control their lives and child-rearing decisions, and offer a constant stream of criticism.

Marital trust, as well as family peace and happiness, requires correcting such parents by requesting that they stop the criticism and communicate more respectfully. Should controlling parents resist such a request, couples may have to protect their marriages by distancing themselves from these parents until they are willing to relate in a more respectful and loving manner.

In addition to correction, forgiveness is needed in families with controlling parents. Brittany found herself in need of forgiving her father-in-law as well as her own father, and she understood that the process could well continue for the rest of her life.

Shawn also recognized that he needed to work on forgiving his father for his critical behavior, and not just toward Brittany but toward him throughout his life.

The Control Compulsion and Divorce

Sometimes even loyal husbands and wives can feel like giving up on a controlling spouse, because they feel burned out by the criticism and the disrespect that has been directed at them. I strongly recommend perseverance. In some marriages, however, where the controlling spouse is not open to correction or change, separation can lead to a "hitting bottom" and a commitment to work on the control compulsion.

In severe cases, spouses seek to divorce a controlling husband or wife. A 2010 study of Minnesotans who filed for divorce showed that growing apart, cited by 55 percent, and not being able to talk together, cited by 53 percent, were the major contributing factors to the decision to divorce.[3]

Controlling and disrespectful behaviors lead spouses to put up walls and to be reluctant to communicate with each other, with the result that they grow apart. Victim spouses often feel insulted or even verbally abused. Often, they also express the desire to protect their children from experiencing such treatment in the home. Chapter 10 describes interventions to protect marriages and children in this dangerous state of marital and family turmoil.

Ongoing Forgiveness

The work of forgiveness toward a parent who severely damaged trust or who modeled controlling behavior can go on periodically for many years. I explain to couples that the work of using past forgiveness exercises, described in chapter 1, may well continue for the rest of their lives,

---

[3] A.J. Hawkins, "Reasons for Divorce and Openness to Marital Reconciliation", *Journal of Divorce and Remarriage* 53, no. 6 (2012): 453–63.

especially at certain times of the year, such as holidays and birthdays, when people often suffer from painful memories. The request for and the giving of forgiveness is an important aspect of maintaining the health of all marriages.

Brittany came to understand that forgiveness is the work of a lifetime. She persevered in forgiving her father and her father-in-law over the course of several years. Shawn also worked on forgiveness. He realized that he, too, needed to forgive his father for criticism that had hurt both him and his wife. He needed to forgive Brittany for all the times she had been dominating, disrespectful, and angry. Both Shawn and Brittany committed to the process of healing and to the cultivation of mutual respect.

The Benefits of Faith

As with selfishness, the major spiritual cause of the need to control is Original Sin. According to the *Catechism*, in the book of Genesis, Adam and Eve demonstrated domineering behavior immediately after the Fall: "Their relations were distorted by mutual recriminations; their mutual attraction, the Creator's own gift, changed into a relationship of domination" (1607; cf. Gen 3:12; 2:22; and 3:16b).

Since the cause is partly spiritual, so must the cure be. Spouses report seeing improvement in their marriages by praying for the healing of childhood wounds and for the freedom from habits they formed by modeling after controlling parents. The regular reception of the Sacraments of Reconciliation and the Eucharist have been reported to be effective in building trust and in resolving intense anger from childhood. Also effective is participation in Catholic programs for troubled marriages, such as Alexander House and Retrouvaille.

Faith is essential in resolving the controlling tendencies that originate in childhood trauma. The *Catechism* accurately identifies the solution to this major marital difficulty: "Without [God's] help man and woman cannot achieve the union of their lives for which God created them 'in the beginning'" (1608).

Faith helps to save many marriages under severe stress. Research at the University of Virginia led by the late Dr. Steven Nock has shown that religious faith reduces severe marital stress and considerations of divorce in three ways. First, faith allows spouses to perceive God as the benefactor and protector of marriage. Second, those with faith recognize a sense of duty to God to develop strong relationships and communication skills. Third, the conviction that marriage is sacred helps to manage severe marital stress, often with great success.[4]

Shawn and Brittany deepened the practice of their Catholic faith in order to heal their marriage through greater mutual respect. They found inspiration for this in Scripture passages such as the following:

> Likewise you husbands, live considerately with your wives, bestowing honor on the woman. (1 Pet 3:7)

> Let each one of you love his wife as himself, and let the wife see that she respects her husband. (Eph 5:33)

> Outdo one another in showing honor. (Rom 12:10)

> So whatever you wish that men would do to you, do so to them. (Mt 7:12)

> Pay all of them their dues ... respect to whom respect is due, honor to whom honor is due. (Rom 13:7)

[4] Steven L. Nock, Laura Ann Sanchez, and James D. Wright *Covenant Marriage: The Movement to Reclaim Tradition in America* (New Brunswick, N.J.: Rutgers University Press, 2008), 112.

Shawn turned to Scripture to help him and Brittany to overcome the fears that were fostering controlling and avoidance behaviors. He related that he was particularly helped by Psalm 56:11: "In God I trust without a fear."

Spouses have also reported being helped by growth in their relationship with Our Lady as their loving and protective mother, as described, for example, by Saint Louis de Montfort in *True Devotion to the Blessed Virgin*.[5] Saint John Paul II had a great devotion to this book and took from it the motto of his papacy: *Totus Tuus* (I am totally yours, Mary). He wrote, "Mary's motherhood, which becomes man's inheritance, is a gift: a gift which Christ himself makes personally to every individual."[6]

John Paul II lost his mother as a young child, his only brother at twelve years of age, and his father at nineteen. With such a history of childhood trauma, compounded by living in a country occupied alternately by two of the most barbaric and controlling political systems the world has ever known, Nazism and Communism, John Paul II might have suffered from severe anxiety and could have developed a need to control others. Yet his strong relationship with Our Lady, as his other comforting mother, protected him from this harmful personality conflict. His life can be an example for those who struggle with anxiety and insecurity, showing them how to maintain a psychologically healthy personality by turning to God in faith and trust.

A good sense of humor can also be helpful in overcoming the urge to control others, by counteracting the tendency to take oneself too seriously and to overestimate

---

[5] Louis de Montfort, *True Devotion to the Blessed Virgin* (Charlotte, N.C.: Tan Books, 2010), 117.

[6] John Paul II, Encyclical Letter *Redemptoris Mater* (March 25, 1987), no. 45.

one's abilities to control outcomes. Gently reminding one's spouse in a loving and cheerful manner, "Remember, the Lord is in control—not you or I" can help to mitigate the effects of fear and insecurity.

4

Responsibility Closes Emotional Distance

The greater the feeling of responsibility for the person the more true love there is.

—Saint John Paul II

Jesus said to Simon Peter, "Simon, son of John, do you love me . . . ?" He said to him, "Yes, Lord; you know that I love you." He said to him, "Feed my lambs."

—John 21:15

The first goal of this chapter is to help spouses understand and learn to address one of the most common complaints expressed by wives and husbands—they feel lonely because they are married to someone who is emotionally distant. The second goal is to help couples understand more fully their responsibility to grow in mature love.

The causes of emotional distance are numerous, but they arise most often from the prevailing view of marriage, in which one is responsible for only one's own happiness and not also the happiness of one's spouse. Another cause is a husband's unconscious modeling after his father's emotionally distant behavior or a wife's mistrust of her husband

Karol Wojtyla, *Love and Responsibility* (San Francisco: Ignatius Press, 1993), 131.

because of hurts from her father or other significant men in her past.

This chapter presents the harm done to spouses by emotional distance as well as the challenging process of uncovering this marital conflict, which many spouses tend to deny. It also explains the virtue of responsibility and describes how it helps to resolve emotionally distant behavior through improving one's thoughts, words, and actions.

Kyle and Carmen

"I love Kyle," Carmen told me, "but sometimes I feel like he really doesn't care about me." Kyle voiced an almost identical complaint. As we talked, both Kyle and Carmen accused each other of not being affectionate, rarely giving compliments, and seeming withdrawn. Carmen said that she thought Kyle was distant and preoccupied with himself and his work. "He thinks that it's my responsibility to take care of everything regarding our children and our home," she said.

A review of their family backgrounds revealed that Kyle's father was a good man who worked hard to provide for his family. When asked whether his primary way of expressing love was deeds, affection, or praise, Kyle responded deeds. He came to recognize that he had modeled after a father who had been emotionally distant as a result of his modeling after his father (Kyle's grandfather), who was the same way. This previously unrecognized personality trait interfered with Kyle's being more emotionally giving and supportive of his wife.

Carmen grew up in large family in which she was like a second mother, assuming many responsibilities for younger siblings. Because of this background, she felt overly responsible for her own five children, and this feeling was compounded by a lack of emotional support from Kyle. Carmen, however, had greater freedom in emotional self-giving than Kyle, because she modeled herself after her warm, affectionate mother. Because Carmen's father had a bad temper, she had difficulty relaxing and feeling safe with Kyle at times, and she realized that in recent years she had been holding back emotionally in the marriage because of feeling neglected by him.

These marital conflicts led to significant sadness and loneliness for both Carmen and Kyle. At times, Kyle sought to escape from his pain through the use of Internet pornography, which led to guilt and more withdrawal from his wife. By the time they came to see me, they were both discouraged and were close to losing hope that their marriage could improve.

Fortunately, both husband and wife wanted to understand all the factors that potentially caused their unhappiness. The two issues that emerged clearly were Kyle's modeling after a father who was emotionally distant and Carmen's fears arising from her father's anger. Both Kyle and Carmen decided to grow in self-knowledge and the virtues that would help break the control that their pasts still exerted over them.

The Harm Caused by Emotionally Distant Behavior

Emotionally distant behavior can cause significant loneliness, sadness, anger, anxiety, and loss of trust in one's spouse. The lonely spouse may come to feel rejected, unloved, tense, and insecure. These emotional responses may also occur in children who witness growing distance and coldness between their parents. Children want to experience a flow of love between their father and mother, which becomes a source of stability, comfort, and trust in their lives.

The wounded spouse may seek to escape from his pain through a variety of compulsive behaviors, including overeating, abusing alcohol or drugs, and using pornography. The wounded spouse is also vulnerable to infatuations that could lead to infidelity. Severely painful loneliness can develop in a neglected spouse and can result in depressive illness with a loss of energy, concentration, and attentiveness and sometimes insomnia.

Sometimes emotionally distant people refuse to admit they are hurting their families. They criticize their spouses for depressive symptoms and resist seeing their role in causing them. Unless the conflicts in the emotionally distant spouse are uncovered and addressed, thoughts of despair or separation or divorce can occur in the wounded spouse, in part to escape from severe emotional pain.

Recognizing Emotional Distance in Marriage

Emotional distance may be denied for many years in marriage, especially during the busy period when children are being raised. Emotional pain cannot be buried indefinitely, however, and will in time emerge.

Here are the common signs of an emotionally distant spouse:

- Excessive time in solitary activity, in front of screens, especially in the evenings and on weekends
- Difficulty in praising
- Difficulty in showing affection

- Avoidance of intimacy
- Irritability and criticalness
- Selfishness
- Controlling behaviors
- Failure to communicate cheerfully and positively
- Lack of appreciation of and attention to the marital friendship
- Avoidance of responsibility for the well-being of one's spouse
- Disordered life priorities, with the placement of work, children, other family members, and recreational activities ahead of one's spouse
- Overly independent behaviors
- Difficulty in relaxing at home with one's spouse

Spouses who are emotionally distant often have great difficulty in accepting this weakness because they believe that they are giving to their loved ones in other ways. These include caring for young children and working hard to provide financially for the family. Therefore, it can be helpful to praise a spouse for showing love through these efforts while asking for improvement in areas on the list above.

Causes of Emotional Distance

Emotional distance in marriage is usually the result of emotional trauma in childhood, modeling after an emotionally distant parent, hurts from previous loving relationships, selfish views of marriage, or marital and family stresses.

Not a small number of men unconsciously model after fathers who related to their wives and to them in an emotionally distant manner. Many of these fathers showed love to their families by working hard to provide for them but had difficulty in communicating to their spouses and children the love, praise, and affection in their hearts.

Most spouses are initially defensive about exploring the possibility that they acquired emotional distance from a parent. They can become more open to this process, however, after first identifying the parent's good qualities that they have imitated and that are benefitting their marriage, such as self-sacrifice, loyalty, and faith.

The most common origin of emotional distance in wives is hurts from their fathers due to their bad temper, selfishness, controlling behaviors, substance abuse, or infidelity. This unrecognized pain can significantly harm a woman's ability to feel safe with her husband, leading her to keep him at a distance. Another origin can be hurts from before the marriage that were caused by relationships with other men. Also, a woman may put up walls between herself and her husband in response to her husband's emotional distance.

While the most common cause of emotional distance is unrecognized and unresolved hurts in the father relationship, emotional distance can also result from the mother relationship, and these hurts are more difficult to heal. The reason is that a loving and comforting relationship with one's mother is essential for establishing the ability to feel safe and to trust. A mother's love provides the foundation for giving and receiving love in later life.

Over the past twenty years, I have seen a significant increase in spouses who lack a secure mother relationship. The leading reason for this is the spread of socially accepted selfishness and a resulting increase in mothers who turn in on themselves and thus damage their emotional sensitivity to their children.

At a marital conference in Manhattan, a young woman related that she thought many of her female friends had trust problems from hurts from their mothers. Their mothers had put themselves and their careers ahead of the needs of their husbands and children, she said.

Women currently initiate almost 70 percent of divorces.[1] While children lose trust in both parents when they divorce, they lose more trust in the parent who files for the divorce. The increase in mother hurts could be related to this increase in women filing for divorce.

Regardless of which parent begins the divorce process, adult children of divorced parents have a deep-rooted fear of being betrayed and abandoned. Divorce scholar Judith Wallerstein wrote that for children of divorced parents, "anxiety about relationships was at the bedrock of their personalities and endured even in happy marriages."[2] Similarly, the death of a child's parent also can lead to an unconscious dread that a similar tragedy could occur in married life. The fear of the loss of one's spouse, either to death or divorce, has led many adults to limit their vulnerability in their marriages, with the result that they come across to their family members as emotionally distant.

Other relationship hurts can also contribute to emotionally distant behaviors. Betrayals and other injuries by siblings, friends, co-workers, and in-laws can damage trust. Wounds from broken relationships with members of the opposite sex can also weaken trust. Once a person loses trust in others, it is difficult for him to keep his heart open, even to a loving spouse.

---

[1] American Sociological Association, "Women More Likely Than Men to Initiate Divorces, but Not Non-Marital Breakups," *ScienceDaily*, August 22, 2015, www.sciencedaily.com/releases/2015/08/150822154900.htm.

[2] Judith S. Wallerstein, Julia M. Lewis, and Sandra Blakeslee, *The Unexpected Legacy of Divorce* (New York: Hyperion, 2000), 300.

The Challenge of Self-Giving

Even without a wounded heart, it is difficult for men and women to commit to the sacrificial, Christlike self-giving that is essential to marriage, especially in a society that has overwhelmingly adopted the idea that one should feel primarily responsible for one's own happiness and only minimally responsible for the well-being of one's spouse. But without a generous self-gift, marital love is difficult to maintain over time.

Many spouses give themselves fully during the early period of their marriage, but after being pummeled by years of stress, unresolved emotional wounds from the past can emerge and create distance. Among the causes of stress are the needs of young children and pressures at work. Both husband and wife can put up self-protective walls to shield themselves from the strains and the pains of life.

During the early years of married life, many couples use contraception to protect themselves from unintended pregnancy. They might believe that postponing pregnancy in this manner will strengthen their marriage. But in fact, contraception can increase selfishness and emotional distance. Men are particularly vulnerable to seeing intimacy solely in sexual terms and feeling entitled to sexual relations. When contraception makes the sexual availability of his wife seem like a given, a man can become less attentive to his wife's needs and less interested in quality time together and regular communication. For her part, his wife can feel as though she is being taken for granted and treated as a sexual object. Feeling angry and resentful, she can pull away from her husband.

Catholic couples benefit from acknowledging that each spouse brings to a marriage special gifts but also weaknesses that make self-giving a challenge and can cause emotional distance. When these weaknesses are uncovered and addressed, by growing in self-knowledge and cultivating the habit of responsibility, emotional distance can be overcome.

The Habit of Responsibility

The first step in the journey toward a healthy marriage is to recognize the need to take responsibility for it. The next step is to make a daily commitment to engage in the hard work of developing mature love. Responsibility is an important virtue that helps spouses to protect and to strengthen their marriages.

In essence, responsibility means fulfilling one's duties toward one's spouse and children by caring for their well-being and encouraging their fulfillment as persons. To modern ears, the word "responsibility" is often associated with heavy and unpleasant burdens, but John Paul II explained the enriching and liberating aspects of responsibility:

> To feel responsibility for another person is to be full of concern, but it is never in itself an unpleasant or painful feeling. For it represents not a narrowing or an impoverishment but an enrichment and broadening of the human being. Love divorced from a feeling of responsibility for the person is a negation of itself, is always and necessarily egoism. *The greater the feeling of responsibility for the person the more true love there is.*[3]

John Paul II also explained:

> There exists in love a particular responsibility—the responsibility for a person who is drawn into the closest possible partnership in the life and activity of another.... Responsibility for love clearly comes down to responsibility for

[3] Woytyla, *Love and Responsibility*, 131. Emphasis in the original.

the person, originates in it and returns to it. This is what
makes it such an immense responsibility.[4]

In a healthy marriage, husband and wife are keenly
aware of the value and the goodness of each other, in
spite of personality weaknesses. They feel a strong sense of
responsibility for their spouse as a gift entrusted to them
by God. Growth in responsibility draws spouses out of
themselves and into the happiness of giving themselves
completely to each other. The more spouses give to one
another, the greater their sense of fulfillment.

Responsibility for one's growth in love requires facing
with humility and courage any personal weaknesses that
could harm one's spouse. Accepting responsibility for the
emotional, relational, and spiritual health of the marriage
strengthens spouses to engage in the challenging struggle of
uncovering and fighting against personality conflicts and
family-of-origin weaknesses that can interfere with mature
marital love. This virtue prevents spouses from turning
inward, expands and purifies their hearts, and helps them
to focus on "we" and not on "me". It protects spouses
from becoming prisoners of themselves.

Responsible husbands and wives try to protect each
other as much as possible from loneliness, anxiety, insecurity, and anger. They try to avoid laying undue burdens
on each other's shoulders. They humbly offer and receive
gentle correction from each other.

Romantic Love, Friendship, and Spousal Love

In *Love and Responsibility*, John Paul II identifies three
major phases of love: *romantic love*, *friendship*, and *spousal
love*. In forty years of practice, I have found it helpful for

[4] Ibid., 130.

married couples to understand these phases in order for them to take responsibility for their relationship.

Romantic Love

While John Paul II did not use the term "romantic love", it fits his description of the early stage of a loving relationship between a man and woman, which is marked by attraction, desire, and sympathy. Romantic love begins when a couple experiences strong feelings of attraction to each other. At first, these feelings simply "happen" spontaneously; they are not chosen or willed.[5] They are based on what appear to be the good attributes of a person, including physical attributes, but they are not yet informed by true knowledge of the other person and are therefore not enough for building a lasting relationship.

Attraction quickly develops into sexual desire, and couples have a responsibility to determine if this early stage of love can become a true friendship before their desires run away with them. "For even those that are not intellectually aware of it may sense that if desire is predominant it can deform love between man and woman and rob them both of it."[6] This determination is particularly urgent at a time when individuals experience enormous pressure to enter sexual relationships even when they do not know if the other person is trustworthy.

Friendship

While romantic love is powerful and important, it is not enough to support a marriage, which John Paul II said needs to be based on nothing less than friendship. The

[5] Ibid., 76.
[6] Ibid., 82.

pope defined "friendship" as "a full commitment of the will to another person with a view to that person's good".[7] In other words, true friends want the best for each other. Marital conflicts can develop when spouses place an over-emphasis on feelings of romantic love and desires for sexual intimacy and fail to attend adequately to building a mature friendship.

Building a friendship requires spending time together, doing things together, and communicating with each other. Over time, friends learn more and more about each other and arrive at mutual understanding, trust, and esteem.

Spousal Love

According to John Paul II, love reaches its fullest realization in betrothed (or spousal) love. This love goes beyond friendship to create a unity of two persons. Its essence is self-giving, that is, the surrender of oneself to another.[8] For a marriage to succeed, a couple needs not only romantic love and friendship but also this spousal love. Here the will is decisive—husband and wife choose to love each other completely and exclusively until death.

Responsibility for Love

The process of moving from romantic love through friendship to spousal love is repeated over and over again in marriage, and spouses who take responsibility for each of these phases can overcome emotionally distant behaviors and make their relationship closer, deeper, and stronger.

[7] Ibid., 92.
[8] Ibid., 96.

Responsibility for Romantic Love

Unless romantic love is protected and enriched, marital friendship and spousal love can be seriously harmed. Taking responsibility for romantic love includes showing physical affection daily, including hugs and kisses when leaving home and returning, and using words of endearment such as "honey" and "sweetie". Offering words of praise and gratitude is also important, as is thinking of one's spouse as a gift from God. Calling to mind the qualities that made one's spouse attractive in the first place is a good mental exercise.

Choosing to be physically close in the evenings and on weekends keeps couples from drifting apart. Having a date night can help with this, but so can simply taking an evening walk or eating a candlelit dinner at home.

Spouses manifest responsibility in romantic love by making a daily commitment to maintain a healthy personality—in other words, working on being the kind of person one's spouse wants to be with. Smiling regularly, being cheerful, offering encouragement and affirmation, avoiding expressions of anger and disappointment, holding back from criticizing and blaming—these remove some of the reasons spouses drift apart.

Responsibility for Friendship

Friendship has the distinctive feature of sharing and sacrificing in common. Spouses can build their friendship by doing things together, shoulder to shoulder. Sitting down to make goals and plans together for the good of the family also builds a spirit of common purpose.

Responsibility for the marital friendship includes growing in self-knowledge about one's weaknesses in giving. Confiding in each other regarding these things can build understanding, compassion, and trust. Committing to protect each other from anxiety, insecurity, and loneliness can turn spouses into each other's champions.

The marital friendship is also helped by reviewing how it is going, communicating areas of growth, and asking how one can improve. Praying together can be a source of encouragement and strength. Many spouses report that they are helped by daily entrusting to the Lord their needs and concerns.

Responsibility for Spousal Love

In my clinical experience, the major causes of difficulties with spousal love are primarily psychological and spiritual. These psychological conflicts interfere with the ability to give oneself completely to one's spouse.

Unlike friendship, marriage is a vocation in which two people make a permanent and exclusive commitment to each other that is expressed in sexual union. The spouses not only give themselves to each other but also open themselves to the gift of children. Marriage therefore requires a greater level of trust and generosity than friendship does.

Various emotional states that may represent unresolved family-of-origin anger, mistrust, loneliness, low self-esteem, or selfishness can interfere with spousal love. When spouses take responsibility to work through these, while maintaining loyalty to the goodness in each other, spousal love becomes stronger.

Obstacles to Responsibility

When couples like Kyle and Carmen report that they feel as though they are drifting apart, I offer them the following checklists to identify the specific things they are experiencing and witnessing in their marriages.

For a Catholic husband, signs and causes of emotional distance include:

- Lack of interest in the romantic side of the relationship
- Failure to build a friendship with his wife
- Placing work, sports, or children before his wife
- Reliance on sexual intimacy to reduce stress and to build confidence
- Insecurity caused by a poor relationship with his mother or father
- Loss of trust in his wife due to her anger, controlling tendencies, or emotionally distant behaviors
- Use of his wife as a sexual object
- Failure to communicate well
- Excessive worries and stresses
- Weak spiritual life
- Poor body image and weak confidence
- Pornography use
- Excessive anger
- Compulsive masturbation
- History of being sexually abused

In a wife, the signs and causes of emotional distance include:

- Loss of closeness due to the husband's lack of interest in the romantic and friendship aspects of the marriage
- Loss of trust in her husband due to his failure to communicate
- Insecurity from a poor relationship with her father or her mother
- Mistrust because of previous romantic relationships or sexual experiences

- Selfishness
- Failure to appreciate the importance of sexual intimacy
- Falsely assuming that it is the husband's responsibility to initiate marital intimacy
- Poor body image and weak confidence
- Contraceptive use
- Weak spiritual life
- Lack of life balance
- Excessive worries and stresses

The Distant Husband

Husbands often lack the awareness of parental weaknesses they have acquired, because such issues are infrequently discussed among males. The commitment to become a more responsible protector of one's spouse, marriage, and children, however, strengthens men to face the ways they are being emotionally distant from their wives.

When a man uncovers the common psychological conflict of having a father who showed his love to his wife and children by deeds but not by praise or affection, he can be motivated to be loyal to his father's good qualities but not to his weaknesses. For some men, however, this process can be challenging, and their wives need courage, patience, and perseverance in requesting more warmth and closeness and an end to repeating a parent's distant behavior.

Men usually desire to be strong and to protect the ones they love, especially their wives and children. Their longing can motivate them to overcome any weaknesses they have modeled after their fathers. An important step in the healing process is for a husband to think about how he can protect his wife's loving heart, on which he and their children depend. He can do this by reflecting on ways he can protect his wife from the harmful effects of loneliness, anxiety, insecurity, the anger of others, and feeling over-whelmed or overburdened.

Men often discover that their lack of self-confidence in caring for the emotional needs of their wives stems from their not knowing a man who modeled this behavior. Their fathers did not show this kind of tenderness to their mothers and therefore did not speak to them about it. These realizations usually result in the emergence of anger with the father and the subsequent need for forgiveness.

Initial steps for taking greater responsibility for one's wife include asking her how she is feeling, actively listening to her concerns, offering positive comments about her efforts on behalf of the family, showing physical affection, complimenting and encouraging her, doing more around the home, spending less time in front of screens, and spending quality time with the children.

If a couple is using contraception, a husband's first step away from this practice is to deepen his understanding of the Church's wisdom on this subject. He could start with the encyclical letter *Humanae vitae* by Pope Paul VI, which predicted that contraception would cause husbands to treat their wives as sexual objects and with a lack of refinement. Another step is for the couple to learn fertility awareness methods of family planning, which result in better communication and deeper trust between spouses.

Husbands who are distant tend to minimize disrespectful behavior in children toward their mother. Their commitment to grow in sensitivity and love for their wives involves insisting that children work to master their anger with forgiveness, their selfishness with generosity, and their attempts to control with respect.

The role of faith is important in helping Catholic husbands to take responsibility for their marriages. Catholic men report that their attentiveness to their wives grows with daily prayer. Also important are the Sacraments of Reconciliation and the Eucharist. Having good role models is essential, and these can be found through participation in Catholic men's groups.

Spouses are also helped by regular church attendance. Marital research has found that married couples who attend church together are significantly more likely to enjoy happy relationships than couples who do not.[9]

The Distant Wife

Wives are often sincerely surprised to discover that their husbands are not the sole cause of their struggles with sadness, anxiety, low self-esteem, and irritability, and that these emotional battles had begun in childhood. Overcoming the emotional distance that has built up between them and their husbands requires uncovering wounds from the past.

Some women spent their childhoods trying to make their parents happy by helping around the house and caring for their siblings. The burdens they felt from a young age were then compounded when they began families of their own. Feeling overwhelmed by their responsibilities, such women sometimes pull away from their husbands, as if their husbands were the source of their burdens.

Healing the emotional wounds left by an overly responsible childhood occurs by letting go and letting God, and by working to forgive parents who may have expected too much. In the process, wives are often surprised to discover

[9] W. Bradford Wilcox and Nicholas H. Wolfinger, *Soul Mates: Religion, Sex, Love, and Marriage among African Americans and Latinos* (Oxford: Oxford University Press, 2016), 139.

that they had at times, unconsciously, resented their husband's needs for affection, friendship, and sexual intimacy.

As a woman learns to let go of feeling excessively burdened, by entrusting herself more and more to the Lord, she can take responsibility for her husband, not as yet another person making demands on her but as the greatest gift God has given her. Greater clarity about his goodness develops, gratitude for him deepens, and trust grows. The ability to communicate in more tender and positive ways begins to unfold.

Carmen had shown her love for her husband primarily through deeds—by caring for their home and their children—but as she took the road toward healing, she understood more fully her responsibility to show her love for Kyle through kind words, affection, and sexual intimacy.

Some wives are emotionally distant from their husbands because of wounds from their fathers or other important men in their past. These hurts can undermine a woman's ability to trust her husband and give herself unreservedly to him. Emotional pain from the past can be resolved through the work of forgiveness, which may need to continue periodically for many years. Communication about this healing process can help to bridge the gap between a wife and her husband and strengthen their friendship.

The role of faith is also beneficial to wives in the healing of their emotional wounds. Turning over to God the anger, the pain, and the fear caused by betrayals and disappointments can bring peace. Confessing excessive anger, resentment, and bitterness in the Sacrament of Reconciliation is a powerful source of healing. This approach is particularly helpful for overcoming the trauma of abuse suffered in the family of origin or in previous relationships.

As with husbands, wives need role models of responsible self-giving in marriage. Friendships with women in healthy marriages can provide helpful encouragement and support. One must be cautious, however, about friendships with women who are in troubled marriages or who do not respect the Sacrament of Marriage. Many Catholic wives report that developing a relationship with the Blessed Mother through prayer is a source of comfort and protection. Meditating on entrusting children and husbands to Our Lady diminishes anxiety and increases a sense of psychological well-being in many wives.

Growing Closer

Identifying their emotionally distant behaviors and uncovering their roots in their families of origin helped Kyle and Carmen to grow closer. By taking responsibility for each other's well-being and fulfillment and for all the aspects of their love, they strengthened their marriage. The process took persistence and hard work, but they found that having a committed love that grows more tender with the passage of time was worth the effort.

5

Trust Calms Anxiety

Do not be afraid to welcome Christ and accept his power.

— Saint John Paul II

Cast all your anxieties on him, for he cares about you.

— I Peter 5:7

The goal of this chapter is to address the most common cause of conflict in marriages and families—anxiety. As with anger, anxiety and its close cousin mistrust are often denied in childhood only to emerge later and be misdirected at one's spouse, children, relatives, friends, and co-workers. Anxiety is also the result of our typically over-scheduled lifestyles. This chapter discusses the harm anxiety causes to marriage, its manifestations, and its origins and describes ways to reduce anxiety by growth in trust. Regardless of the numerous ways anxiety harms families, a healing path exists for mastering it by building trust.

Tiffany and Alec

Tiffany twisted a tissue as she spoke. I could tell from the haunted expression in her eyes that she wasn't sleeping

John Paul II, homily, Saint Peter's Square (October 22, 1978).

well. During our session, it became apparent that she was suffering from intense anxiety. She felt overwhelmed by pressures and the lack of balance in her life. She longed for earlier times in her marriage when she and her husband, Alec, had more time together for their friendship. His work was demanding and took far too much of his time.

Troubling Tiffany even more were the demands being made on her family by her four children's numerous year-round athletic activities, including traveling sports teams. She felt overwhelmed by the constant driving to practices and games as well as the long weekend tournaments. "All this time in sports is robbing us of family time, especially on the weekends," she said. She regretted that family dinners, relaxing Sundays at home, and date nights with her husband had become things of the past.

Tiffany was angry with Alec for failing to be more sensitive to her needs and for not protecting her and the children from excessive outside demands. She wanted him to stop helping their children's coaches, but he refused to do so. From her point of view, Alec had lost his sense of priorities, and as a result, her ability to trust him was diminishing. "I just can't go on like this," she said, battling back tears. "I think that I'm going to have a breakdown or choke Alec!"

Anxiety: Prevalence, Nature, and Symptoms

Anxiety is a major source of irritability, sadness, conflict, and unhappiness in married life. In fact, it is the most common psychiatric disorder in adults and youth. A Harvard Medical School study in 2007 found that, over the course of the previous year, about 19 percent of U.S. adults suffered from an anxiety disorder, with a higher prevalence of anxiety among females (23.4 percent) than males (14.3 percent).[1] The same study estimated that 31.2 percent of U.S. adults experience an anxiety disorder at some time in their lives.[2] In 2006, at least 27 million Americans took medications for anxiety and depression, twice as many as those who did in the mid-1990s.[3]

Just as anger can be appropriate or excessive, so can anxiety. Appropriate anxiety is a beneficial emotional reaction that warns us of danger. It can be a helpful indicator that we need to take some action to protect ourselves or our loved ones from harm. On the other hand, excessive anxiety is a detrimental emotional overreaction to minor stresses. Associated with the loss of the ability to feel safe, anxiety can lead to a loss of trust in one's spouse.

Loss of trust can jeopardize a marriage because trust is the basis for giving and receiving marital love. Feeling unsafe triggers a fight-or-flight response. A wife might withdraw from her husband or fight him in anger, or she might fluctuate between both of these extremes. Intensely angry reactions associated with a loss of trust are a leading cause of harm to marriages and families. Under duress, spouses begin to focus more on each other's weaknesses than on each other's goodness.

Excessive anxiety can present itself in a wide range of intense and debilitating emotional, cognitive, behavioral, and physical symptoms. Among these are disrupted sleep,

[1] Harvard Medical School, "Twelve-Month Prevalence Estimates", National Comorbidity Survey, https://www.hcp.med.harvard.edu/ncs/ftpdir/NCS-R_12-month_Prevalence_Estimates.pdf.

[2] Harvard Medical School, "Lifetime Prevalence Estimates", National Comorbidity Survey, https://www.hcp.med.harvard.edu/ncs/ftpdir/NCS-R_Lifetime_Prevalence_Estimates.pdf.

[3] M. Olfson and S. Marcus, "National Patterns in Antidepressant Medication Treatment", *Archives of General Psychiatry* 66, no. 8 (August 2009): 848–56, https://doi.org/10.1001/archgenpsychiatry.2009.81.

increased fatigue, and irritable bowel syndrome. Under duress, spouses can focus more on each other's weakness than on each other's goodness. Often an anxious spouse will withdraw from physical intimacy.

Over time, a generalized anxiety disorder can develop. Generalized anxiety disorder is one of the most common clinical diagnoses of anxiety. It is a state of chronic worry, defined as excessive anxiety occurring more days than not for at least six months. Symptoms can include restlessness or feeling keyed up or on edge, being easily fatigued, and having difficulty controlling irritability. It can also involve problems in concentrating, muscular tension in different parts of the body, and sleep disturbance. The physical symptoms can be irritable bowel syndrome with diarrhea, abdominal pain, rapid heart rate, muscular spasms in different parts of the body, dizziness, nausea, shortness of breath, numbness and tingling, chills or hot flashes, and feelings of unreality.

Anxiety also causes spiritual harm. Saint Francis de Sales accurately described the dangers of anxiety in his *Introduction to the Devout Life*:

> With the single exception of sin, anxiety is the greatest evil that can happen to a soul. Just as sedition and internal disorders bring total ruin on a state and leave it helpless to prevent a foreign invader, so also if our heart is inwardly troubled and disturbed it loses both the strength necessary to maintain the virtues it had acquired and the means to resist the temptations of the enemy. There is nothing that tends more to increase evil and to prevent enjoyment of good than to be disturbed and anxious.[4]

[4] Francis de Sales, *Introduction to the Devout Life*, trans. John K. Ryan (New York: Doubleday Image, 1989), 251–52.

Anxiety Checklist

Couples like Tiffany and Alec benefit from reviewing the following checklist of behaviors caused by anxiety.

- Intense irritability
- Controlling behaviors
- Sadness and loneliness
- Catastrophic thinking (fear that something bad is going to happen)
- Social insecurity and isolation
- Emotional overreactions to minor life events
- Lack of cheerfulness
- Compulsive habits (to try to diminish anxiety)
- Excessive fears, including fear of one's responsibilities
- Emotional rigidity or withdrawal
- Intermittent severe mistrust
- Substance abuse
- Compulsive sexual behaviors
- Withdrawal from physical intimacy

Severe Anxiety

Severe anxiety can lead a person to think that his spouse is not trustworthy. This distorted way of thinking results in increased feelings of irritability toward a spouse. In marriages, anxiety, like anger, needs to be addressed regularly, rather than denied, in order to prevent strong mistrust from developing and undermining the relationship. Saint Paul wrote that we should not allow the sun to go down on our anger (see Eph 4:26); the same applies to our anxiety.

Symptoms of severe mistrust include the following:

- Failure to treat one's spouse as one's best friend
- Inability to see the goodness in one's spouse

- Regular overreactions in extreme anger toward one's spouse and children
- Sadness and a lack of cheerfulness
- Harsh, disrespectful speech
- Preoccupation with worries that pull one away from one's spouse and children
- Insomnia
- Difficulty in giving praise
- Excessive criticism
- Numerous psychosomatic symptoms, including dizziness, muscle spasm, and diarrhea
- Thinking one's spouse is not trustworthy
- Difficulty in receiving help or advice
- Inability to trust one's children
- Difficulty in giving praise and love to one's spouse
- Failure to consult one's spouse in making important decisions
- Inability to trust one's spouse with the children
- Difficulty in trusting God

Causes of Anxiety

A major cause of anxiety in married life is a weakening of confidence. When confidence drops, insecurity grows, resulting in anxiety. Numerous factors can trigger a drop in confidence, particularly if there is severe stress in the present or unresolved insecurity from the past.

Causes of Anxiety in Childhood and Young Adulthood

For many spouses, anxiety does not begin in married life but rather in youth. Damage to trust, confidence, and hope for loving relationships can develop at one stage of life, be denied and buried, and then emerge later. Many people sincerely believe that their anxiety is solely caused by a spouse, when, in fact, they entered their marriage with a serious unrecognized weakness in trust.

The development of basic trust is the first state of psychosocial development, occurring, or failing to occur, early in life. Success in childhood produces feelings of security, confidence, and optimism, whereas failure leads to anxiety, insecurity, and sadness. The ability to trust others is a robust predictor of happiness in life because it protects one's basic ability to feel safe, which is essential for successful interpersonal relationships.

The foundation for trust and feeling safe as an adult depends first and foremost on events in early childhood, particularly a close, loving relationship with one's mother. This relationship is essential to establishing the basic ability to trust and to feel safe. Fortunately, most spouses in my experience have had stable mother relationships, although this is changing due to harmful cultural trends that encourage selfish individualism at the expense of generous self-giving.

Most spouses who did not have a close mother relationship will have difficulties later with anxiety and with trusting their spouses, children, in-laws, and others. Yet we are not meant to be prisoners of our childhood wounds. Our loving God provides sources of healing for emotional wounds, although a great deal of courage, humility, and strength are needed to admit the truth of childhood pain and to engage in the hard work of acquiring virtues, especially trust, that can decrease anxiety and fears of betrayal.

In my clinical experience, unconscious hurts from the father relationship are the most common family-of-origin cause of anxiety and mistrust, weaknesses in confidence, and loneliness in childhood and adulthood. As with mother wounds, spouses with father mistrust tend to deny or make light of their pain and instead blame their spouse exclusively for anxiety or unhappiness.

Growing up in a home with serious conflicts between the parents or with separation or divorce creates intense anxiety and fears in children. This psychological pain is a major cause of the retreat from marriage and of anxiety and difficulty in trusting one's spouse. Also, the harsh treatment of one parent by the other can lead to a fear of being treated in a similar manner, which can cause an aversion to marriage.

Another cause of anxiety is modeling unconsciously after an anxious and insecure parent. Damage to trust can also arise from hurts caused by siblings. In these cases, siblings misdirected at one another their anger at a parent. Other past experiences that can damage trust are repeated family moves, a serious and prolonged medical or psychiatric illness in a parent, the death of a parent, or serious childhood illness.

Another common source of anxiety in youth and young adults is hurts from peers and previous loving relationships. The hookup culture has damaged the ability of many adolescents and young adults to trust, because they have given themselves repeatedly to others who were neither caring nor trustworthy. Dr. Miriam Grossman, a clinical psychiatrist formerly practicing at the University of California–Los Angeles, has documented the damage done particularly to young women who have been treated repeatedly as sexual objects.[5] For not a small number of wives, trauma from previous sexual relationships can impair their ability years later to give themselves in romantic love, friendship, and spousal love to their husbands.

---

[5] Miriam Grossman, *Unprotected: A Campus Psychiatrist Reveals How Political Correctness in Her Profession Endangers Every Student* (New York: Sentinel Press, 2007), 13–30.

Rather than being quick to blame each other for anxiety and lack of trust, couples should reflect upon their foundation in trusting and feeling safe based on their experiences in childhood. The following are important question to consider:

- Did your parents treat each other and you in a loving and respectful manner?
- Could you have modeled after a parent who had difficulty with mistrust and insecurity?
- Might trust in the marriage have been weakened by hurts from other important people in your life or your spouse's life before you met?
- Do you and your spouse believe that you had good foundations to trust in each other based on your family background?

Causes of Anxiety in Married Life

Trust diminishes and anxiety increases when spouses do not treat each other in a respectful, sensitive, and loving manner. Other common causes of anxiety are insecurity, which leads to the need to control, and the failure to master anger or to establish life balance. An excessive sense of responsibility and financial worries can also cause anxiety, as can serious problems with children, in-laws, and friends. Substance abuse or illness in either spouse can strain a marriage.

Growing hostility toward Judeo-Christian beliefs and values, particularly toward Catholicism, is a growing cause of concern. Many Catholic spouses report feeling distraught and helpless because of attacks on the traditional family and their faith. A history of abortion can also harm trust, particularly if no healing has occurred through the Sacrament of Reconciliation and programs such as Project Rachel, a post-abortion apostolate.

Economic hardships are a significant source of stress and anxiety in marriages. Many husbands feel overly anxious about their ability to meet their current financial responsibilities, much less put aside money for their children's college education. In addition, changes in the workplace have intensified fears about job security. These include an undue pressure for profits; a marked decrease in loyalty between employers and employees; the firing of long-term, loyal employees; the failure to treat employees with respect; and unreasonable performance expectations, such as the demand that employees be constantly available to respond to work-related issues.

Anxious and mistrustful spouses should ask themselves if they believe that the major sources of fear in their marriages is current external forces, unresolved hurts before the marriage, or both. Upon serious reflection, they find that the answer is usually both.

Many spouses mistakenly believe that having knowledge of childhood or premarital hurts and previously discussing them with friends, a therapist, a support group, or one's spouse is sufficient to heal these wounds. But although self-knowledge is vital, it is inadequate to overcome childhood hurts that result in intense anxiety. Self-knowledge must be complemented by a daily commitment to forgive those who have damaged trust before the marriage, especially the parent one trusted less. Anger, which is present in all psychiatric disorders, must be uncovered and resolved, or it will interfere with recovery from anxiety.

The Habit of Trust

Trust can be understood in marriage as confidence in the character, goodness, value, reliability, fidelity, and loyalty of one's spouse. Placing trust in a spouse is, to a certain degree, an act of faith. When trust in a spouse is shaken by various stresses or disappointments, knowledge of how to restore trust is essential to the marriage and to the psychological and physical health of the spouses.

Trust is essential to life and to all human interactions. Without it, life would be intolerable and marriage unlivable. Although there may be times when our trust in someone is misplaced (if a person is not trustworthy) or is disappointed (when someone fails to honor our trust in some way), we still need to trust others.

For Catholic spouses, trust means relying on the Lord's protective love. Spouses do this through prayer and the sacraments, particularly the Sacraments of Reconciliation and the Eucharist. Studies have demonstrated that religious faith is effective in diminishing the severe anxiety that can harm trust in marriages. It is also crucial in the recovery of marital trust after it has been weakened.

Trust enables spouses to think and feel that their husbands or wives wish the best for them and to believe that they will do what is expected of them in married life. While trust must be given, trust also must be earned by each spouse trying to think and to act with the good of the other in mind.

The powerful romantic feelings early in a loving relationship are not a clear indication that the person loved is, in fact, trustworthy. Only as the couple's friendship progresses is it possible to make this vital appraisal. Often, however, men and women rely excessively on their romantic feelings and base their decisions on them. They need to hold their feelings in check and allow the friendship phase of the relationship to grow, allowing the real beauty and goodness of the person to be revealed. Only then can lasting confidence in the loved one grow, leading to a deeper friendship that is no longer based solely on romantic attraction or physical attractiveness.

Friendship and trust are deepened by a shared vision and mission and by regular church attendance. Trust is sustained, in part, by acting in a loving, virtuous, self-giving, mature, and responsible manner. The failure to maintain a healthy personality during times of stress is a major reason for the loss of trust in married life.

All spouses bring a degree of weakness in trust into their marriages, because no one has perfect parents, siblings, and peers, nor has anyone been perfectly trustworthy himself. Fortunately, spouses can grow in trust and trustworthiness regardless of past hurts and failures before or during their marriage, provided they make a commitment to grow in these areas. For example, spouses can work on establishing the healthy priorities of God first, spouse second, and children third. Excessive time outside the home that disrupts family quality time and regular family dinners should decrease. The result is less stress in the home and less anxiety in everyone.

Spouses can grow in trust first by recognizing how vital it is to their happiness. Next, they can commit to fighting against anxious or mistrustful thinking patterns (referred to in the mental health field as "cognitive distortions") and anxious emotional and behavioral responses, particularly when stressed. Negative thinking patterns include the following:

- My spouse is not reliable or trustworthy and never was.
- My spouse does not wish the best for me.
- I should not share my worries with my spouse.
- Something terrible is going to happen (catastrophic thinking).

- There is no hope for my anxious feelings.
- My spouse could betray me.

These negative thoughts can be conquered and replaced with trust if the following steps are consciously chosen each day:

1. See the goodness of one's spouse.
2. Engage in regular, positive communication.
3. Show affection.
4. Affirm each other's gifts.
5. Seek the right balance.
6. Forgive.
7. Set a good example.

See the Goodness of One's Spouse

While a daily commitment to see the goodness of one's spouse will not completely heal anxiety from past hurts caused by parents or others, it should diminish the tension arising from current stresses. Spouses are encouraged to think about, and to be grateful for, the goodness and the gifts in each other and to write them down in a journal. Through this process, they come to see their spouse's weaknesses as being on the periphery of their goodness and not as defining characteristics.

Of course, reducing mistrust also depends on a spouse's trying to act in a more trustworthy manner, which often requires resolving family-of-origin and other premarital weaknesses and receiving loving correction from one's spouse. A daily decision to see the goodness in one's spouse does not mean denying his predominant psychological weakness (everyone has at least one) or failing to correct and to ask for growth in virtue. After a loving and gentle correction, an apology and a commitment to change is essential in building trust and in reducing anxiety.

Engage in Regular, Positive Communication

Regular, positive communication is vital for building trust in a marriage. The daily commitment to offer positive, cheerful, affirming messages protects love and helps it to grow. It also decreases worry and stress.

The proverb that marital problems (or worries) that are shared are halved is psychologically correct, provided they are communicated in a sensitive, respectful way, without excessive anger and criticism. Worries and anxieties that are not faced and discussed build up and can lead to discouragement and sadness. In fact, anxiety often precedes the development of depression, especially in adolescents.[6]

Spouses do not need to have all the answers to the problems they discuss, and they do not need to agree about everything, but they do need to listen to each other attentively and lovingly and to respond in an affirming way. Spouses should not remain silent when spoken to, as this could be received as a sign of indifference, disrespect, quiet anger, or mistrust.

When offering one's spouse a needed correction or a recommendation for growth in addressing a weakness, one should begin and end by affirming his goodness. This approach is described as the sandwich technique of correction. To avoid causing anxiety and discouragement,

[6] K. R. Merikangas, J. P. He, M. Burstein, S. A. Swanson, S. Avenevoli, L. Cui, C. Benjet, K. Georgiades, and J. Swendsen, "Lifetime Prevalence of Mental Disorders in U.S. Adolescence: Results from the National Comorbidity Survey Replication—Adolescent Supplement", *Journal of the American Academy of Child and Adolescent Psychiatry* 49, no. 10 (October 2010): 980–89, https://doi.org/10.1016/j.jaac.2010.05.017.

spouses should give each other five positive comments for each negative one. When one spouse has a severe mistrust wound from the past and overreacts consciously or unconsciously in anxiety, anger, and controlling behavior, the other spouse should offer a gentle reminder that he is trustworthy and loyal and request more trust.

Not infrequently, spouses discover that they have not trusted each other or the Lord enough with their marriage and their problems. Many also have failed to communicate what they need from their spouses. Apologizing for these mistakes can assist in deepening communication and trust.

Show Affection

The First Letter of John states, "Perfect love casts out fear" (4:18). Although love between spouses is never perfect, marital affection decreases anxiety and relieves stress by providing a significant degree of comfort. Affection to and from children has a similar beneficial effect. Physical affection and warmth are as important as food, water, and sleep for the health and well-being of spouses and children. Affection builds trust, and trust manifests itself in affection.

A common difficulty related to intimacy in marriage is modeling after an emotionally distant parent, as was addressed in the first chapter. This weakness will need to be identified and resolved, in large part through forgiveness exercises, in order for the spouse to grow in the trust needed for emotional self-giving.

Affirm Each Other's Gifts

A lack of confidence can arise when one's gifts have not been appreciated, and this, in turn, causes anxiety. This kind of anxiety is associated with the obsessive and excessive concern about how one is viewed by others. Most spouses bring a degree of insecurity into their marriages, and expressions of praise and gratitude can help in overcoming it.

Spousal affirmation and praise cannot, however, completely heal insecurities caused by an overcritical or distant parent, bullying trauma, rejections in previous relationships, or excessive pressure and criticism in the workplace. These kinds of hurts will generally require repeated decisions to forgive in order to stop the recurring memories that bring sadness and a lack of confidence.

Seek the Right Balance

Excessive worries regarding finances, children, extended family, and care for the home can be major sources of anxiety, mistrust, and irritability. Anxiety can also develop from the failure to establish proper priorities. Finding balance in one's life, therefore, is vital for reducing anxiety.

The development of schedules for everyone in the family can be essential for making sure that the important things in life happen. In the process, many spouses discover disordered priorities in the family's use of time. Likewise, the development of budgets can bring runaway spending under control, allowing for saving and for charitable giving and lessening financial worries.

The anxiety caused by a lack of balance diminishes when couples take control of their time and money. By placing God first, their spouse second, and their children third, the important things in life come into view. In many families today, children's activities and desires have become the tail wagging the dog. Putting those in the right perspective is essential to relieving anxiety.

Forgive

Anxiety is associated with high levels of irritability. The anxious spouse may deny or minimize the presence of anger often because of the intensity of the feelings of anxiety. The anger that develops after a hurt, which causes an increase in anxiety, can encapsulate anxiety. This anger can both block the resolution of anxiety and contribute to its returning.

Studies by Dr. Robert Enright and his colleagues at the University of Wisconsin–Madison have demonstrated that forgiving those who inflicted hurts decreases anxiety, sadness, and anger and increases self-esteem.[7] The resolution of anger with those who have inflicted unjust hurts, through forgiveness, is necessary to resolve underlying anxiety.

Spouses are encouraged to make a daily commitment to forgive those who damaged their safe feeling or trust in life. The request for forgiveness from one's spouse for hurts of the past also helps strengthen trust, as does the commitment to be more forgiving and to avoid overreacting in anger.

Many spouses will not experience significant reduction in anxiety and mistrust until they have engaged in the hard work of forgiving the parents or significant others who disappointed them the most. These hurts from the past can be so strong that often the most effective approach to such anger is spiritual forgiveness, in which the person reflects, "I am powerless over my anger and want to turn it over to God" or "Lord, take my anger" or "God, forgive my [parent, spouse, or significant other] until I can."

[7] Robert D. Enright and Richard P. Fitzgibbons, *Forgiveness Therapy: An Empirical Guide for Resolving Anger and Restoring Hope* (Washington, D.C.: American Psychological Association, 2014).

Overreactions in anger toward a spouse or children need to stop in order to protect them from anxiety. While this may seem almost impossible for some spouses, it can be accomplished by working diligently on immediate forgiveness exercises, described in chapter 1.

Set a Good Example

Parental modeling of trust and calmness in the home, especially during times of stress, is essential in the healthy formation of children. Also, the avoidance of expressions of anger between spouses is vital in protecting children from anxiety and catastrophic thinking that their parents may divorce.

Parental modeling of trust and calmness in the home, especially during times of stress, is essential in the healthy formation of children. Parents have a serious responsibility to work to resolve any marital conflicts in order to prevent divorce, which causes anxiety in children. Even expressions of anger between spouses should be avoided so as to protect children from worry that their parents may divorce. Moreover, teaching children how to address anxiety with trust is important for their development.

The Importance of Faith

A number of studies have shown that religious practice can be helpful in reducing anxiety. One survey of thirty-seven thousand men and women found that those who attended church, synagogue, or other religious services often had lower prevalence of depression, mania, and panic disorder. The lead researcher, Dr. Marilyn Baetz of the University of Saskatchewan, stated, "Higher worship frequency was associated with lower odds of both current and past depression, [and] current and past mania."[8] Another study demonstrated the importance of religion as a predictor of improvement in panic disorder after one year.[9]

Catholic spouses struggling to regain trust have found the practice of their faith very helpful, especially the Sacraments of Reconciliation and the Eucharist. Their very marriage is a sacrament of the Church, meaning a source of grace. Every time they give themselves to each other—in the marital embrace; in serving, forgiving, and bearing with one another; in praying with and for each other—they experience the love of Christ.

Catholic couples have also discovered the tremendous peace of mind that comes through prayerful meditation. The more spouses entrust the Lord with their marriage, the less fear they have in facing and discussing problems. Honest discussions are more fruitful when couples give their concerns to the Lord before and after their conversations. The following meditative prayer has been reported to be helpful: "Lord, I trust you with our marriage. I am confident in you. Help me to trust you and my spouse more and more each day." This meditation has been particularly helpful for spouses with deep wounds from controlling, angry, addicted, distant, or selfish parents, from parental divorce, and from abuse trauma.

Tiffany and Alec increased their trust in God and each other through a devotion to the Divine Mercy, as revealed to Saint Faustina. They regularly prayed the Chaplet of

[8] M. Baetz, R. Bowen, G. Jones, and T. Koru-Sengul, "How Spiritual Values and Worship Attendance Relate to Psychiatric Disorders in the Canadian Population", *Canadian Journal of Psychiatry* 51, no. 10 (September 2006): 657.

[9] R. Bowen, M. Baetz, and C. D'Arcy, "Self-Rated Importance of Religion Predicts One-Year Outcome of Patients with Panic Disorder", *Depress Anxiety* 23, no. 5 (2006): 266–73.

Divine Mercy and meditated upon the Divine Mercy image with the words "Jesus, I trust in you."

Pope Emeritus Benedict XVI reminded Catholic spouses that increasing their trust in God can diminish anxiety. He wrote:

> In the face of the broad and diversified panorama of human fears, the Word of God is clear: those who "fear" God "are not afraid".... To be without "fear of God" is equivalent to putting ourselves in his place, to feeling we ourselves are lords of good and evil, of life and death. Instead, those who fear God feel within them the safety that an infant in his mother's arms feels (cf. Ps 130:2). Those who fear God are tranquil even in the midst of storms for, as Jesus revealed to us, God is a Father full of mercy and goodness. Those who love him are not afraid.[10]

Numerous Scripture passages from the book of Psalms and the New Testament help to reduce anxiety and stress. My father, who was the third of five children and whose father died when he was five years old, said he was greatly encouraged by these words of Jesus when he was raising his family:

> Consider the lilies, how they grow; they neither toil nor spin; yet I tell you, even Solomon in all his glory was not clothed like one of these. But if God so clothes the grass which is alive in the field today and tomorrow is thrown into the oven, how much more will he clothe you, O men of little faith! (Lk 12:27–28)

Tiffany and Alec also found courage in Scripture. They listened to these words of Jesus: "Let not your hearts be

---

[10]Benedict XVI, Angelus, Saint Peter's Square (June 22, 2008).

troubled; believe in God, believe also in me" (Jn 14:1). They applied Saint Paul's advice about not letting the sun go down on their anger (see Eph. 4:26) to their challenges with anxiety, by entrusting God with the worries of the day at bedtime, as the psalmist says, "Cast your burden on the LORD, and he will sustain you" (Ps 55:22).

Strong faith lessens anxiety and associated emotional overreactions that occur from feeling overwhelmed and worried, modeling after a parent's anxiety or catastrophic thinking, being traumatized by parents' divorce or conflicts, and experiencing severe stress with children, work, or extended family relationships.

6

Hope Reduces Sadness and Loneliness

But if we keep our eyes fixed on the Lord, then our hearts are filled with hope.

—Saint John Paul II

May the God of hope fill you with all joy.

—Romans 15:13

The goal of this chapter is to address loneliness, sadness, and depressive illness in married life. The origins and the manifestations of strong feelings of sadness are presented, as are ways to reduce them.

The causes of emotional and mental pain are not always clear. Consequently, married people may incorrectly think that their pain is solely the result of disappointments with their spouses. The truth may be, however, that a person's sadness may arise from other sources, such as unresolved sadness from a past relationship. Mistrust, anxiety, anger, and low self-esteem, all of which contribute to depressive illness, may also have been present before marriage.

John Paul II, Address to Young People in New Orleans (September 12, 1987), no. 12. Emphasis in the original.

Although people sometimes benefit from seeking professional help to deal with depressive illness, one thing they can do for themselves is cultivate the virtue of hope. Faith and hope are not the same thing, but there is a link between them. "Faith is the assurance of things hoped for, the conviction of things not seen" (Heb 11:1). In other words, faith in God's love gives us the assurance that we will obtain through Christ the tender mercy we need and hope for. Such confidence is the antidote to despair. This chapter does not seek to present religious practice alone as a cure for serious mental illness, but to show that it can be a source of comfort for those who suffer from sadness.

Marital Conflicts and Depression

Research has demonstrated that an unhappy marriage is a risk factor for the development of depression. A major study from Yale University found that spouses in unhappy marriages were associated with a twenty-five-times-higher risk of depression than those in untroubled marriages.[1] Another study found a tenfold increase in risk for depressive symptoms associated with marital discord.[2]

Spousal anger has been found to be a contributing factor to depressive illness in the other spouse; the more the angry husbands in the study exhibited hostile and antisocial

[1] Myna M. Weissman, "Advances in Psychiatric Epidemiology: Rates and Risks for Major Depression", *American Journal of Public Health* 77, no. 4 (April 1987): 447.

[2] K. Daniel O'Leary, Jennifer L. Christian, and Nancy R. Mendell, "A Closer Look at the Link between Marital Discord and Depressive Symptomatology", *Journal of Social and Clinical Psychology* 13, no. 1 (1994): 33–41, https://doi.org/10.1521/jscp.1994.13.1.33.

behavior, the more depressed their wives were after three years. This research also showed that warm, positive behavior from husbands lessened the negative impact of their hostile behavior.[3]

Anthony and Carla

Carla was driven to seek help for several reasons. She not only struggled with intense sadness but also suffered from fatigue, insomnia, irritability, and loneliness. Although she was taking an antidepressant, her symptoms had not diminished much.

Initially she believed that her sadness was caused primarily by conflict with her husband. She felt that Anthony was oblivious to her needs for loving and supportive attention, affection, and communication. She thought he gave more of himself to their four children, his job, and his interests than to her. He seemed not to understand her desire for a closer relationship with him. She said, "If he were more sensitive to me and was meeting my needs, I would not be feeling this terrible sadness and loneliness."

Anthony, like many spouses, could have been more aware of his responsibility to protect his wife from sadness and loneliness, and he could have been a more positive, cheerful communicator. He could have also been more attentive to his wife's desire for a closer relationship. Yet he was often so drained by the pressures of his work that he could not meet Carla's emotional needs when he returned home at the end of the day. While there was room for

[3] C. M. Proulx, C. Buehler, and H. Helms, "Moderators of the Link between Marital Hostility and Change in Spouses' Depressive Symptoms", *Journal of Family Psychology* 23, no. 4 (2009): 540–50.

improvement in his sensitivity to his wife, the truth is, he was not the only cause of Carla's depression.

It is important to uncover negative thinking, or cognitive distortions, in depressed spouses. Negative thinking is signified by thoughts like these:

- My spouse is the sole cause of my sadness.
- My spouse can't change and therefore can't help me with my pain.
- I will not be able to be happy in my marriage because of my spouse.
- My family background does not play a role in my sadness and anger.
- Nothing will improve our marriage
- I am responsible for my own happiness.

To help Carla understand that Anthony was not the sole cause of her unhappiness, she was asked if she could trace any of her sadness to her family background or to hurts prior to their marriage. She said that she did not enjoy a close, warm, loving relationship with her mother, and she came to understand that her mother had modeled after Carla's maternal grandmother, who was selfish and unaffectionate. Carla also said that she wished she had a more comfortable relationship with her father, who was often anxious.

The loneliness Carla experienced because of the distance she felt between herself and her parents was deeply buried, but during treatment it came to light. Her experience was not unusual. Often in treatment, after reviewing family history, spouses suffering from sadness will comment, "I had no idea that I have struggled with loneliness since I was young."

Reviewing family history also helped Anthony. He recognized that he was acting like his father. His dad traveled a great deal for his job and worked on projects around the house on Saturdays. On Sundays he relaxed, but not in ways that included other members of the family. Anthony did not see his father communicate a great deal with his mother, show her affection, or offer her praise. He realized that at times he might have unconsciously repeated these behaviors toward Carla.

Fortunately, Carla and Anthony were motivated to improve their marriage. Anthony committed himself to being more sensitive to his wife's needs and doing more to protect her from loneliness and sadness. Carla agreed to stop blaming Anthony exclusively for her pain and to become more aware of the other sources of her sadness. Both husband and wife sought to forgive the family members who had hurt them or whose faults they had unwittingly imitated. They also made an effort to grow in the virtue of hope.

Prevalence of Depressive Illness

About 17 percent of the U.S. population (roughly 20 percent of women and 13 percent of men) will suffer from a major depressive disorder, a severe and long-lasting form of depression, in their lifetime.[4] The incidence of depression has increased over the past fifty years. At least 27 million Americans take antidepressants, twice the number of those who did so in the mid-1990s.[5] Suicidal thoughts

[4] Harvard Medical School, "Lifetime Prevalence Estimates", *National Comorbidity Survey*, https://www.hcp.med.harvard.edu/ncs/ftpdir/NCS-R_Lifetime_Prevalence_Estimates.pdf.

[5] M. Olfson and S. C. Marcus, "National Patterns in Antidepressant Medication Treatment", *Archives of General Psychiatry* 66, no. 8 (August 2009): 848–56, https://doi.org/10.1001/archgenpsychiatry.2009.81.

and acts have also increased markedly. From 2000 through 2016, the age-adjusted suicide rate increased 30 percent nationwide. For women, it increased 50 percent; for men, 21 percent.[6]

Symptoms of Sadness and Loneliness

Everyone feels sad from time to time. It is a normal emotional response to disappointment, hurt, and loss. Chronic, intense sadness, however, is not normal. It could be a sign of depressive illness. Other sings of depression include insomnia, lack of energy, loss of appetite, poor concentration, and impaired memory. A depressed person might also suffer from a loss of interest in previously enjoyable activities, irritability, and crying episodes.

Being overly quiet or withdrawn and wearing a sad expression can be signs of depression, as can seeking comfort by excessive drinking, eating, and shopping. Depressed people can suffer from sexual disorders, such as compulsive use of pornography and masturbation. Depression can also be manifested in chronic pain and psychosomatic illness.

Sadness and Marriage

Particularly troubling for a marriage is when a sad husband or wife is unable to give cheerfully to the other spouse. This can seriously undermine the ability of the spouses to

---

[6] Holly Hedegaard, Sally C. Curtin, and Margaret Warner, "Suicide Rates in the United States Continue to Increase", NCHS Data Brief, no. 309 (Hyattsville, Md.: National Center for Health Statistics, 2018), 2, https://www.cdc.gov/nchs/data/databriefs/db309.pdf.

communicate positively with each other and to enjoy each other's company. Romantic love, marital friendship, and sexual intimacy all suffer, and a wedge begins to grow between the spouses. Some depressed people can even develop jealousy over their spouse's affection toward their children.

Serious marital conflicts can arise when a sad husband or wife blames the other spouse—often inaccurately—for all the unhappiness, as Carla did for a time. As a result, anger and mistrust can develop toward a fundamentally good, loyal, but not perfect spouse like Anthony. A sad husband or wife can push away a loyal spouse through irritability or criticism, which results in even greater loneliness.

In an attempt to escape from serious emotional pain, a spouse may become emotionally vulnerable to someone else and initiate a separation or a divorce. Earlier in my practice, divorces and separations were more often initiated by unhappy men. Now, however, I am seeing an increasing number of depressed women filing for separation or divorce.

Origins of Sadness and Depression

Couples who want to save their marriage from the effects of sadness need to uncover its origins. While there are hereditary and biological aspects to depressive illness, hurts from the past and ongoing hurts in the marriage can be contributing factors.

Hurts from the Past

Often spouses are unaware that they have some family-of-origin loneliness and sadness, which can emerge with various circumstances and stresses in married life. They can also have blind spots about unresolved hurts that arose in previous important relationships.

The leading family-of-origin cause of sadness is unresolved hurts in the father relationship. With rare exceptions, fathers love their children as much as they can. When their main "love language" is the deeds they do to provide for their families, however, they are often short on words of praise and physical signs of affection. Many children experience this behavior as emotionally distant and long for a closer relationship with their fathers.

The next-most-common family-of-origin cause of sadness is a mother who was controlling, angry, emotionally distant, anxious, depressed, or selfish. Unfortunately, an increasing number of mothers are affected by what has been described as the narcissism epidemic. Narcissism (extreme selfishness) turns people in on themselves. In women, it damages their natural inclination toward nurturing their children.

Another cause of sadness is trauma related to the divorce of parents. Divorce deprives children of the stability and the comfort they receive from being loved by a united father and mother. Children yearn to be drawn into the flow of love between their parents, which dries up during and after a divorce. Also, when parents withdraw their love from one another, the children doubt their parents' ability to love them. Only a father and a mother committed to love one another can provide children with the greatest assurance that their love for them will not fail. Parents' divorce causes profound sadness and mistrust in children, who often unconsciously take these wounds into their own marriages.

Other causes of unconscious sadness are hurts and disappointments in significant relationships before marriage, such as those with siblings, peers, and romantic interests. A Harvard Medical School study of 229 men revealed that poorer relationships with siblings prior to age twenty and a family history of depression independently predicted both the occurrence of major depression and the frequency of use of mood-altering drugs by age fifty.[7] Spouses have also reported sadness resulting from growing up in a two-child family, in which they did not have a desired brother or sister, or in which they yearned for more siblings.

It is vital for married people to understand that the love they receive from their spouses, no matter how strong and comforting, cannot completely resolve the loneliness and the sadness from a past unmet emotional need for love. When people are motivated to grow in self-knowledge and in the awareness of previous hurts, however, they can work on resolving the wounds that cause them sadness in their marriage.

Marital Hurts

Married people who seek help with feelings of sadness also need to identify the hurts they have suffered from their spouse. For many couples, a lack of friendship with each other is a leading cause of loneliness. There is simply not enough communication, affirmation, and affection in their relationship, often because the spouses do not spend enough time with each other. Sometimes a lack of life balance is to blame for this. But people can also become sad when a spouse is angry, controlling, emotionally distant, anxious, or critical. We all are hardwired to have warmth, love, and praise flow in our direction. We naturally feel sad when we are at the receiving end of criticism, coldness, or contempt.

[7] R.J. Waldinger, G.E. Vailant, and E.J. Orav, "Childhood Sibling Relationships as a Predictor of Major Depression in Adulthood: A 30-Year Prospective Study", *American Journal of Psychiatry* 164, no. 6 (June 2007): 949–54, http://doi.org/10.1176/ajp.2007.164.6.949.

Some spouses, particularly wives, experience recurrent and intense sadness because they want to have more than one or two children and their husbands will not respect their desire to share more in God's creative love. This sadness is often associated with anger when a spouse who resists having more children is perceived to be motivated by selfishness and insists upon using contraception.

Other Causes of Sadness

Additional causes of sadness in family life are the serious problems of a child or a close relative. Among young people there is a documented increase of narcissism and its associated anger and poor impulse control.[8] As a result, many marital and family therapists are seeing a related increase of depression in parents, particularly mothers, who are harried by and worried about the behavior of their children. Another source of disappointment and anxiety occurs when a child away at college abandons the faith and morals of his parents and adopts self-destructive behaviors.

Some spouses are lonely and sad because of an absence of close friends. Stay-at-home wives and mothers are particularly vulnerable to this, especially when they live in a neighborhood where most women work outside the home. On the other hand, some mothers who work full-time report sadness due to long separations from their young children.

Other causes of sadness are the stresses of life, such as job pressures and financial worries. Struggling with anxiety is mentally and emotionally draining, predisposing people to sadness and depression. Of course, biological factors can play a role in a person's response to stress, as can the behavior that was modeled by one's parents.

[8] Jean Twenge and W. Keith Campbell, *The Narcissism Epidemic: Living in the Age of Entitlement* (New York: Aria Books, 2009).

The frenetic pace of modern life has no doubt contributed to the stress level in people's lives. Many Christian mental health professionals (and I am one of them) also blame chronic stress on the eclipse of religious practice, which once gave meaning and purpose to people's lives and was a refuge from anxiety.

Without a religious foundation for their marriage, many couples lack a sense of common mission. For centuries, marriage meant fulfillment through self-giving and self-denial for the sake of one's spouse and children. Particularly in the Catholic Sacrament of Matrimony, there was the added pursuit of holiness (rather than wealth) and the goal of attaining eternal life together.

Religion provides not only a purpose for marriage but also a source of support when spouses experience difficulties. Personal and family problems can cause intense anxiety, insecurity, and sadness. But these emotions can be greatly relieved by meditative prayer and reliance on divine providence. Saint John Paul II wrote about the spread of depressive illness in modern society and the spiritual life that is needed to address it:

> *The spread of depressive states has become disturbing.* They reveal human, psychological and spiritual frailties which, at least in part, are induced by society. It is important to become aware of the effect on people of messages conveyed by the *media* which exalt consumerism, the immediate satisfaction of desires and the race for ever greater material well-being. It is necessary to propose new ways so that each person may build his or her own personality by cultivating spiritual life, the foundation of a mature existence.[9]

[9]John Paul II, address on depression (November 14, 2003), no. 2. Emphasis in the original.

152

Contraception and Depression

Instead of cultivating spiritual life as the foundation of one's existence, many people have chased after material prosperity while leaving a spiritual vacuum in their lives. In doing so, many couples have resorted to contraception to limit the size of their families. Yet newer research demonstrates a relationship between hormonal contraceptive use and increased risk of depression and suicide, the symptoms of hopelessness that prosperity purportedly prevents.

A 2016 study of more than one million women living in Denmark found that "use of hormonal contraceptives was associated with subsequent antidepressant use and first diagnosis of depression at a psychiatric hospital.... Adolescents seemed more vulnerable to this risk than women 20 to 34 years old."[10] A second study of nearly a half million Danish women found that those who used hormonal contraceptives had a greater risk of suicide than those who did not. Again, adolescents experienced the highest relative risks. The authors of the studies concluded, "Considering the severity of these little-recognized potential side effects of hormonal contraceptives, health professionals and women starting hormonal contraceptives should be informed about them."[11] Given this research, when identifying sources of sadness in married women, contraception should be investigated as a possible factor.

[10] Charlotte Wessel Skovlund, Lina Steinrud Mørch, Lars Vedel Kessing, and Øjvind Lidegaard, "Association of Hormonal Contraception with Depression", *JAMA Psychiatry* 73, no. 11 (November 2016): 1154–62, http://doi.org/10.1001/jamapsychiatry.2016.2387.

[11] Charlotte Wessel Skovlund, Lina Steinrud Mørch, Lars Vedel Kessing, and Øjvind Lidegaard, "Association of Hormonal Contraception with Suicide Attempts and Suicide", *American Journal of Psychiatry* 175, no. 4 (November 2017): 336–42, https://doi.org/10.1176/appi.ajp.2017.17060616.

Healing Sadness through Hope

Mental health professionals employ several approaches to help spouses who suffer from chronic, intense sadness. These include cognitive-behavioral therapy, marital therapy, insight-oriented psychotherapy, and positive psychology. Medication is also often used in treating depressive illness. These approaches, or some combination of them, can sometimes produce positive results, but they require the oversight of mental health experts. Hope is also a strong remedy for sadness, and it can be practiced by anyone.

On the natural level, hope is the confident desire of reaching a future goal that is difficult to attain. Applied to marriage, hope involves believing that a fulfilling relationship with one's spouse is possible, desiring this relationship, and then taking the necessary steps to attain it.

The Church teaches that, on the supernatural level, hope is a theological virtue given by the Holy Spirit in the Sacrament of Baptism. "Hope is the theological virtue by which we desire the kingdom of heaven and eternal life as our happiness, placing our trust in Christ's promises and relying not on our own strength, but on the help of the grace of the Holy Spirit" (CCC 1817). Although the theological virtue of hope is a gift, as are the other two theological virtues of faith and charity, it grows stronger with exercise.

Both natural and supernatural hope promote belief in a positive outcome to difficult events and circumstances in one's life. They help to keep one's heart open to both giving and receiving love, the only way spouses can fight against and endure periods of sadness or loneliness. Hope diminishes the discouragement that can cause spouses to give up on their marriage.

Hope is cultivated when spouses daily commit to the goal of improving their marriage. With their thoughts,

words, and actions, spouses can choose to hope in themselves, in each other, and in their marriage. They can think,
speak, and act with the confidence that their efforts to love
and support each other better will make their lives better.

Hope and Healing Family-of-Origin Hurts

Hope can be directed at healing wounds from the past.
Once these hurts are uncovered, spouses can think several times daily, "I hope that by forgiving my parent who
disappointed me and by not misdirecting my anger with
my parent at my spouse, my sadness will decrease." When
spouses forgive those who have hurt them, their sadness
does indeed decrease, along with their anger and anxiety.
Consequently, their marital relationships usually improve.

Working on the primary parental wound helps spouses
feel less depressed, lonely, irritable, and mistrustful. Subsequently, they appreciate more all the ways in which their
spouses' love and loyalty helps them. They also come to
recognize, however, that marital love alone cannot resolve
the sadness and the loneliness experienced in the past. To
expect otherwise is unreasonable. A husband or a wife who
discovers that feelings of disappointment have resulted
from unreasonable expectations should request forgiveness from the other spouse.

Most parent-child relationships improve after the grown
child marries, but one that does not improve can be an
ongoing source of sadness for the adult child. Sometimes
the source of the problem is the parent's interference in the
adult child's marriage or offensive behavior toward the adult
child's spouse. An effective approach for this difficulty is first
to work on forgiving the parent and then to offer gentle but
clear correction of hurtful behavior.

Initially, spouses often do not feel like forgiving an
offending parent, but they become motivated to do so

when they realize that without forgiveness their sadness will not be resolved. For deep hurts, forgiveness with the mind (cognitive) or with the heart (emotional) seems impossible. Fortunately, when this occurs, most spouses can employ spiritual forgiveness by giving their anger to the Lord several times a day, which usually brings about significant emotional relief. Catholic spouses also find it helpful to take anger and resentment toward an offending parent to the Sacrament of Reconciliation on a regular basis, not because these emotions are sinful, but because the graces of the sacrament help to overcome them.

In our book on the treatment of excessive anger, *Forgiveness Therapy* (2014), Dr. Robert Enright and I explained that, to recover from depressive illness, it is essential to resolve the anger associated with sadness. Contrary to the thinking that influences many mental health professionals and marital therapists, sadness is not anger turned inward. These powerful emotions are related, however.

Anger arises most often from the sadness of an unjust hurt. Then anger can encapsulate the sadness from our past hurts. The result is that spouses, in a sense, can be emotional prisoners of their past hurts. Forgiveness decreases both the anger and its associated sadness.

Hope and Healing Marital Hurts

Discouragement about marriage can diminish and hope can grow when spouses understand the origins of the struggle with sadness and decide together to do something about it. Depressed spouses often feel that others are not sensitive enough to their emotional pain, deepening their feelings of loneliness. When one becomes aware of the causes of sadness in his spouse and embraces a plan for addressing it, the depressed spouse experiences the hope that better days lie ahead. As husband and wife work together, trust between them grows, which strengthens hope even more.

We see in the book of Genesis that God does not intend for us to be alone: "Then the LORD God said, 'It is not good that the man should be alone; I will make him a helper fit for him'" (2:18). Reflection upon this passage strengthens our faith in the plan God has made to protect his children from loneliness in marriage. It builds our hope that by working to improve our marriage, our loneliness can diminish.

Working to improve marriage requires taking responsibility for the relationship and for the well-being of one's spouse. It means striving to protect one's spouse from emotional pain, particularly loneliness. Sadly, many married people assume that they are responsible for only their own happiness and not that of their husbands or wives. This distorted view of marriage arises from the major enemy of marital love—selfishness, which needs to be rejected in the healing process.

Saint John Paul II warned that selfishness can lead to an exaggerated autonomy. He mentioned that in marriage there can be "a mistaken theoretical and practical concept of the independence of the spouses in relation to each other". At the root of many problems in marriage, he wrote, "there frequently lies a corruption of the idea and the experience of freedom, conceived not as a capacity for realizing the truth of God's plan for marriage and the family, but as an autonomous power of self-affirmation, often against others, for one's own selfish well-being."[12]

The acceptance of responsibility for one's spouse helps to correct overly independent thinking and behavior.

---

[12] John Paul II, Apostolic Exhortation on the Role of the Christian Family in the Modern World *Familiaris consortio* (November 22, 1981), no. 6.

Spouses who realize that they have been operating autonomously of the other spouse should request forgiveness. If selfishness has been the reason for refusing to have more than one or two children, that too should be confessed.

Spouses need to appreciate that a generous, sensitive, loving heart makes a person particularly vulnerable to the damaging effects of loneliness and other causes of sadness. In other words, the very tenderness that makes one's spouse so lovable could also make one's spouse prone to hurt feelings. When married to a sensitive person, one needs to commit to being more present to one's spouse; to being a more positive, cheerful communicator; to asking how one could be more helpful. Of particular benefit is asking forgiveness for times of insensitivity and offering words of encouragement, saying with confidence that sadness and loneliness are passing storms in life that give way in time to greater happiness and fulfillment.

As with healing hurts from the past, forgiveness is key to healing hurts from a marriage. Emotional pain decreases when the sad spouse forgives the other for a lack of sensitivity or emotional support. The sad spouse also feels better by asking forgiveness for blaming the other exclusively for his unhappiness. As anger decreases through forgiveness, the hearts of both spouses are softened, and they experience greater warmth and affection for each other. Hope for a better marriage increases.

The Role of Faith

Many studies have demonstrated the beneficial effects of faith in strengthening hope and counteracting depression. While religious practice alone is not a cure for serious mental illness, there is, for example, a correlation between faith and the incidence of suicide. A 2016 study found that women who attend religious services weekly have a much lower risk of suicide than women who do not practice a religion. The 6,999 Catholic wives in the study who went to Mass more than once per week never attempted suicide.[13] This study does not prove that practicing Catholics never contemplate or attempt suicide—we know that they sometimes do—but it does indicate that practicing one's faith strengthens hope for living.

In a systematic review of 850 studies, higher levels of religious involvement were positively associated with indicators of psychological well-being and with fewer incidences of depression, suicidal thoughts and behavior, and drug or alcohol abuse.[14] In another survey, 37,000 men and women who frequently attended church, synagogue, or other religious services enjoyed a lower prevalence of depression, mania, and panic disorders than those who did not.[15] One psychological explanation for these findings is that when people rely on another source of strength besides themselves—namely, on a loving and protecting God—they feel less anxious and more hopeful and confident.

Faith also contributes to marital happiness. A 2016 study found that married couples who attend church together are significantly more likely to enjoy happy relationships

[13] T.J. VanderWeele, S. Li, A.C. Tsai, I. Kawachi, "Association between Religious Service Attendance and Lower Suicide Rates among U.S. Women", *JAMA Psychiatry* 73, no. 8 (August 2016): 845–51, https://doi.org/10.1001/jamapsychiatry.2016.1243.

[14] A. Moreira-Almeida, F.L. Neto, and H.G. Koenig, "Religiousness and Mental Health: A Review", *Brazilian Journal of Psychiatry* 28, no. 3 (September 2006): 242–50.

[15] M. Baetz, R. Bowen, G. Jones, and T. Koru-Sengul, "How Spiritual Values and Worship Attendance Relate to Psychiatric Disorders in the Canadian Population", *Canadian Journal of Psychiatry* 51, no. 10 (September 2006).

than couples who do not regularly attend.[16] The regular practice of religion has been shown to be associated with greater marital stability, higher levels of marital satisfaction, and an increased likelihood that an individual will be inclined to marry.[17] A major study that drew on nationally representative data with twelve measures of marital quality demonstrated that having a religiously committed spouse is positively associated with a variety of affirmative marital outcomes.[18]

Catholic married couples can practice their faith and increase their hope and happiness in a number of ways. The Sacrament of Reconciliation has been discussed with respect to healing hurts from both the past and the present. Frequent Communion also quiets negative emotions that arise in everyday life.

Saint John Paul II's devotion to Our Lady has inspired many Catholics to discover the benefits of developing a relationship with her. Marian devotion is especially helpful for spouses who have brought an unconscious sadness into their marriage from an unmet emotional need for maternal love.

Depressed spouses have reported growth in hope through prayer and meditation. Meditating on Saint Joseph as protector and provider of the Holy Family and on the providential love of God the Father can help spouses struggling with financial worries and hurts from their own fathers.

---

[16] W. Bradford Wilcox and Nicholas H. Wolfinger, *Soul Mates: Religion, Sex, Love, and Marriage among African Americans and Latinos* (Oxford: Oxford University Press, 2016), 139.

[17] A.J. Weaver, J.A. Samford, V.J. Morgan, D.B. Larson, H.G. Koenig, and K.J. Flannelly, "A Systematic Review of Research on Religion in Six Primary Marriage and Family Journals, 1995–1999", *American Journal of Family Therapy* 30, no. 4 (2002): 293–309.

[18] Samuel Perry, "Perceived Spousal Religiosity and Marital Quality across Racial and Ethnic Groups", *Family Relations* 65, no. 2 (April 2016).

Children of divorce have reported feeling less sad and anxious by cultivating a relationship with the Holy Family.

Hope is psychologically healing and liberating. "It keeps man from discouragement; it sustains him during times of abandonment; it opens up his heart in expectation of eternal beatitude. Buoyed up by hope, he is preserved from selfishness and led to the happiness that flows from charity" (*CCC* 1818). A daily commitment to grow in hope is essential for healthy marriages and families.

7

Gratitude Builds Confidence

Remember the past with gratitude, . . . live the present with
enthusiasm and . . . look forward to the future with confidence.

—Saint John Paul II

Give thanks in all circumstances.

— 1 Thessalonians 5:18

This chapter looks at the benefits of maintaining confidence in one's gifts—in marriage, family life, friendships, and places of employment. Its first goal is to help spouses uncover and understand conflicts with insecurity arising from both the past and the present. This chapter describes the harm that insecurity inflicts on marriage, particularly the manner in which it limits mature self-giving to one's spouse and one's children. It presents the benefits of maintaining healthy Christian confidence as well as the numerous manifestations of weakness in confidence. It also explains growth in the virtue of gratitude as a method of strengthening and protecting confidence.

John Paul II, apostolic letter *Novo millennio ineunte* (January 6, 2001), no. 9.

Zeke and Sally

Sally was very happy and fulfilled during the first ten years of her marriage to Zeke. Beginning in year eleven, however, Zeke became increasingly negative, irritable, critical, and aloof. He was not as loving or communicative as he had been. He was less patient at home and easily frustrated with his two children and his tasks around the house. Sally felt that she was slowly losing her best friend and that she could no longer make him happy.

After much thought and prayer, Sally gathered the courage to talk with Zeke about the changes she was seeing in his behavior and to ask him what was wrong. When he responded negatively, telling her that he had no problems, she realized that perhaps he did not understand what was happening to him and the impact it was having on their marriage. This insight helped her to move beyond blaming herself and to look elsewhere for the source of their difficulties.

As Sally considered her husband's behavior, she realized that Zeke was showing signs of losing confidence in himself. While noting that he had been complaining about his work and saying that his employer did not appreciate his efforts, another light came on. She thought, "Zeke has never been able to please his father either."

Sally suggested to Zeke that his frustrations at work seemed to be the cause of his current unhappiness. She also asked if his feelings about his boss could be related to his feelings about how his father had treated him when he was young. Zeke agreed that his problems at work were the root of his troubles. But he said he did not see how his father had any connection with his current situation. He added, "Honey, I think you may be trying to analyze me a little too much." He admitted, however, that his father was difficult to please and that he wished he had a better relationship with him.

Benefits of Confidence

Confidence in our God-given gifts and fundamental goodness makes us comfortable and fulfilled in giving love to our spouse and children and in receiving love from them. The same applies in our relationships with relatives, friends, neighbors, and employers.

Confidence decreases anxiety, irritability, and sadness, while enhancing cheerfulness, an important attribute in married life. Confidence increases our ability to see the goodness in others and to value their opinions, making us good team players rather than overly independent loners. It leads to being less threatened by the talents of others, and it decreases excessive competitiveness, which can harm relationships with spouses, family members, and co-workers. It reduces the need for the attention and the approval of others and lessens our preoccupation with our appearance.

Confidence helps to decrease feelings of envy and worries about our financial status. It helps us to be less stressed in dealing with the challenges of life. It strengthens our courage to rely on divine providence and to resist the pressures to conform to values contrary to our faith in Christ.

Signs of Weakness in Confidence

Lack of confidence needs to be uncovered and addressed to protect marriages and children from its harmful effects. In our clinical experience, deep insecurity is seen far more often in husbands than in wives, primarily because fathers tend to have much greater difficulty in giving praise and affirmation to their sons than mothers do in affirming their daughters. This reality is highly significant because acceptance by one's unconscious role model, the parent of the same sex, is vital in the development of a child's positive sense of self.

Here are some of the signs that point to an inner struggle with insecurity:

- Strong need to prove oneself
- Regular criticism of one's spouse
- Social anxiety and avoidance
- Attempts to be independent of one's spouse
- Anxiety, irritability, and sadness at home and at work
- Limited ability to compliment
- Perfectionistic thinking
- Lack of affection
- Excessive self-criticism
- Preoccupation with the impression one makes on others
- Tendency to be overly quiet or withdrawn
- Preoccupation with the opinion of others
- Tendency to be overly concerned about financial success or bodily appearance
- Extreme competitiveness, including with one's spouse
- Lack of enthusiasm
- Inability to correct one's children or one's spouse
- Numerous compulsive behaviors, including substance abuse, using others as sexual objects, gambling, and pornography addiction
- Inability to communicate the faith
- Flirtatiousness
- Unfaithfulness to one's spouse

Most of these weaknesses can be overcome. First, though, let's look more deeply at the origins of insecurity.

Origins of Insecurity

Numerous stresses in childhood and in married life can wound the development and the maintenance of healthy confidence and result in struggles with insecurity, which are often unconscious. Spouses suffering from a lack of confidence should explore the degree to which their need for a loving and affirming relationship was experienced with each parent, with siblings, and with childhood peers. This understanding is essential, since psychological research has shown that most adult psychological conflicts and disorders begin in childhood.[1] In my forty years of work with hundreds of couples, I have seen that overcoming insecurity in spouses requires the resolution of unconscious or unresolved conflicts in the past. Along with this effort is the need to uncover issues in the present that weaken confidence.

Childhood Origins

The leading childhood hurt that is uncovered in my work with spouses is the lack of an affirming, close, accepting, loving relationship with the father. Over the past twenty-five years, however, we have witnessed a major increase in the lack of a secure, loving mother relationship. Other childhood origins of weakness in confidence include a lack of acceptance by and closeness to siblings or peers.

[1] J. Kim-Cohen, A. Caspi, T.E. Moffitt, H. Harrington, B.J. Milne, and R. Poulton, "Prior Juvenile Diagnoses in Adults with Mental Disorder", *Archives of General Psychiatry* 60, no. 7 (2003): 709–17, https://doi.org/10.1001/archpsyc.60.7.709.

Uncovering the hurts of the past is challenging because most spouses prefer to minimize the emotional pain caused by their families and to focus on marital issues. This is particularly true of husbands who often are not accustomed to discussing and successfully working through emotional struggles.

A child's sense of secure attachment and psychological well-being is first dependent on affection, comfort, praise, and warmth in the mother relationship. Fortunately, most mothers are naturally warm and loving, but we are seeing an increasing number of adult children whose mothers were selfish and distant.

The secure relationship with one's father is also important to the development of confidence. Fathers who are emotionally distant, critical, irritable, difficult to please, alcoholic, selfish, or unfaithful to their wives harm their children's confidence. That confidence is undermined even more if one's father abandons his family.

In regard to long-lasting trauma in the father relationship, Sigmund Freud told an early biographer, Ernest Jones, about the confidence wound he bore from his relationship with his father. Freud related that when he was seven years old, his father became very angry with him and stated, "That boy will never amount to anything." About this event Freud said, "This must have been a terrible affront to my ambition, for allusions to this scene occur again and again in my dreams, and are constantly coupled with enumerations of my accomplishments and successes, as if I wanted to say: 'You see, I have amounted to something, after all.'"[2]

---

[2] Ernest Jones, *The Life and Work of Sigmund Freud*, ed. Lionel Trilling and Steven Marcus (Garden City: Anchor, 1961), 15.

Wives are generally more fortunate with respect to secure attachment to their unconscious role models, their mothers, than husbands are to their role models, their fathers, because mothers tend to be close to their daughters. While the mother relationship is also essential for the psychological health of men, and important for their ability to trust and to respect their wives, it is not as important as the father relationship for the development of their confidence.

When mothers have strong, controlling personality traits, they can harm the development of confidence in their children, who often respond by distancing themselves to escape the disrespectful pressure. This response, however, often results in the development of an unrecognized need for comforting maternal love, which spousal love alone cannot heal.

Husbands with controlling mothers slowly come to understand that they are angry with their fathers for being too weak to curb the disrespectful behavior of their wives. They also resent that they were deprived of a strong male role model in the home, which later interfered with their self-esteem as husbands and fathers.

A positive factor in the development of healthy confidence is growing up with a mother and a father who love each other, have a low level of conflict, and form their children in the virtues that develop character. The flow of love between a father and a mother, which Saint John Paul II described as an icon of the love of the Trinity, provides a sense of well-being and security in children, which is vital in establishing healthy confidence.

The love of only one parent or of parents who are not committed to each other, as in the case of divorce or cohabitation, does not meet a child's needs for secure attachment and leaves the child vulnerable to developing emotional, cognitive, and relational difficulties.

Divorce seriously harms a sense of identity, especially in sons whose fathers leave the marriage. A father's infidelity can also harm a boy's sense of self. A young man confided to me that he had always looked up to his father until he discovered that his father was being unfaithful to his mother. From that day, he no longer respected his father and began to search for another role model, which he was unable to find. The lack of a role model crushed his confidence and resulted in problems with school, work, relationships, and addiction.

There are others besides parents who have an impact on the development of a person's confidence. Angry, critical, or distant behaviors in an older sibling can seriously harm a child's self-esteem. The absence of close and accepting friends of the same sex can result in children feeling inadequate and thinking that something must be wrong with them. In my clinical experience, difficulties in the development of healthy relationships with siblings and peers have increased significantly as a result of the marked increase of selfishness in society, which plays a major role in cyber bullying and bullying in school.

From an early age, children are subjected to the prevailing cultural view that boys need to be good at sports and muscular while girls need to be sexually alluring like actresses and magazine models. Young people are under tremendous pressure to measure up to false standards of beauty, and they suffer from low self-esteem when they fail to do so.

Adolescents are told by many voices that they should be sexually active at their age. Using others as sexual objects is considered a normal, even expected, behavior. Yet sexual experimentation causes serious shame and guilt. Being used sexually and then cast aside leaves deep wounds and shatters confidence.

Adult Origins

Low confidence brought into married life can be compounded by marital conflicts. Insensitive words and behaviors from one's husband or wife is a major cause of insecurity. Furthermore, a person might respond to such treatment by unconsciously modeling after a parent with strong insecurities.

Insecurity and its associated fears can create great difficulties in work by impairing decision-making, attentiveness, concentration, and relationships with bosses and co-workers. These symptoms are often mistaken for attention disorders, and insecure spouses are often more comfortable in attributing their work difficulties to a disorder than in facing their lack of confidence.

Here are some other causes of low confidence:

- Lack of a close marital friendship
- Anger, emotional distance, and criticism from a spouse
- Controlling behaviors by a spouse or other family members
- Lack of spousal affection and intimacy
- Excessive reliance on work or appearance for confidence
- Feeling overly responsible
- Severe financial stress
- Excessive anxiety and criticism at work
- Materialistic thinking
- Weak faith or loss of faith
- Excessive reliance on someone outside the marriage for confidence
- Modeling after an insecure parent

Many Christian spouses report a weakening of their confidence as a result of the growing hostility from media, schools, and branches of government toward the traditional Judeo-Christian, and particularly Catholic, view of marriage, family, unborn life, and the elderly.

Harm from Insecurity

Insecurity can seriously interfere with cheerful self-giving in marriage. It can undermine romantic love, friendship, and spousal love between husband and wife. In an unconscious attempt to escape from the emotional pain of insecurity, many spouses engage in compulsive behaviors, including overeating, substance abuse, pornography, gambling, and excessive exercise. In extreme cases, insecurity can lead to infidelity.

Strong feelings of insecurity make a person vulnerable to extreme anxiety, which can cause irritability, sadness, and ultimately depression. One of the criteria for establishing the diagnosis of a major depressive episode is a feeling of worthlessness.

Spouses suffering extreme lack of confidence can be very difficult to please and are often easily frustrated with themselves and with their spouses. They frequently use excessive criticism, manipulative communication, and controlling behaviors in an unconscious attempt to build their self-esteem. Their insecurity also leads them to distance themselves from family members and friends. This can result in a kind of paralysis that blocks a person from offering opinions, tolerating the views of others, and seeking employment or a better job. It can also lead to excessive quietness, reclusiveness, and avoidance of addressing important issues.

In my clinical experience, I have found that severe insecurity is a leading reason why married men, and increasing numbers of married women, are unfaithful to their spouses.

They may make false accusations against their spouses, blaming them for their anxiety and unhappiness, and may even pursue divorce.

Unconsciously, insecure people use flirtation to boost their self-esteem and build their confidence. They can develop sexually compulsive behaviors, such as obsessive use of pornography. Insecure men and women wear masks to cover their true feelings, and most people have no idea how tormented they are.

A lack of confidence can interfere with parenting and at times can completely block a person's ability to give his children the correction that is essential for their development. The inability to correct is especially found in the face of selfish, angry, defiant, and disrespectful behaviors in children as well as in a spouse. Insecure parents also experience difficulty in teaching their children about the virtue of chastity and the dangers of using people for sexual pleasure.

Gratitude Decreases Insecurity

When gratitude is practiced daily, it is a powerful antidote to insecurity and low self-esteem. It makes sense that in giving thanks for something, a person is acknowledging its value. When a person gives thanks for himself, he is esteeming himself.

A person exercises the virtue of gratitude by being thankful for all the good things he has, including his talents, his family members, and his friends. He acknowledges that his very life is a gift and recognizes its inestimable value and fundamental goodness. By being thankful in this way, a person feels better about himself and his circumstances and is able to face his difficulties with greater confidence.

Gratitude for one's childhood is an important exercise, particularly because the most severe damage to confidence usually occurs when one is young. A person begins by being thankful for the gift of his life, which he received through his parents. Next, he is thankful for all the good things he received in childhood, including a sound mind, a healthy body, his siblings, and the food on the table.

In married life, it is important for spouses to express their gratitude for each other every day. This counteracts the tendency to take one's spouse for granted.

In order to be grateful for everything in one's life, one must address a thinking error or cognitive distortion—the assumption that one must be perfect in all that he is and does. "Don't let the perfect be the enemy of the good" is a wise saying, and people suffering from perfectionism need to remind themselves that they are good and gifted and cherished by others even with their flaws, which everyone else has too.

Appreciation of Male and Female

With so much gender confusion today, it can help to observe that men and women have different attributes and that the unique contributions of both sexes are equally valued and needed by the family and the society at large.

In his apostolic letter on the dignity of women, Saint John Paul II coined the term "feminine genius".[3] Jutta Burggraf, the late professor of theology at the University of Navarre, summarized this genius as "a special capacity to show love, a delicate sensitivity to the needs of others, a special capacity for the other and understanding of inner

---

[3] John Paul II, Apostolic Letter on the Dignity and Vocation of Women *Mulieris dignitatem* (August 15, 1988), no. 31.

conflicts in others".[4] Nature has endowed woman with this special capacity in order to fulfill the role of mother. Man, on the other hand, Burggraf explained, is biologically designed for fatherhood. His "greater distance from the process of gestation and birth enables him to act more calmly on behalf of life; he acts to protect life and guarantee its future; he is a father in a physical and spiritual sense and he is called to be strong, firm, reliable and trustworthy."[5]

Recognizing the unique gifts of men and women creates delight in marriage as it helps husbands and wives to be more thankful for each other. It also builds confidence, assuring spouses that they are providing vitally important and irreplaceable roles in their families.

Although the affirmation and the gratitude that spouses give to each other is essential for a happy marriage, spouses with weak confidence sometimes rely too much on the other spouse as the source for their self-esteem. As pressures and responsibilities grow—for example, when children come along—love from a spouse might not be able to decrease insecurity as it once did. Although the realization that spousal love cannot fully heal deep insecurities can initially be upsetting, it is also liberating. This liberation from excessive dependence on a spouse can then lead to a greater openness to dependence on God. As Saint Augustine famously wrote, our hearts are restless until they rest in God.

Forgiveness and Confidence

Forgiveness can increase the confidence that has been battered by hurts and disappointments. Anger encapsulates all

---

[4] Jutta Burggraf, "Commentary on the Relationship between Men and Women", *L'Osservatore Romano*, February 23, 2005, p. 6.

[5] Ibid.

emotional pain and blocks its healing, which is why for-giveness is so powerful in maintaining a healthy personality and a healthy marriage.

Difficulty in admitting that weakness in confidence is the result of a challenging parental relationship or another life hurt received in childhood is very common, because this pain has often been denied for years. It can be easier to blame a spouse for the unhappiness caused by one's insecurity. In fact, the sadness that one experiences as a result of insecurity coupled with denial of its origin can lead to behaviors that harm that person, his spouse, and his children. Among these are escapist compulsive be-haviors such as pornography use, workaholism, and sub-stance abuse. Excessive exercise to obtain a perfect body can also be a sign of low self-esteem. If lack of confidence is not addressed, it can lead to infidelity, separation, and divorce.

I gently warn such spouses that the failure to resolve the hurts from their families of origin can result in their being emotional prisoners of their past. Understanding the hurts caused by parents or other family members can increase compassion for them, which helps in forgiving them. The same is true for injuries suffered in school or at work. Iden-tifying and forgiving these can decrease potentially harmful anger and insecurity.

In my practice, spouses are asked to reflect on their lives and to draw up a list of all those who have ever harmed their confidence. Then they imagine themselves wanting to understand and to forgive them, using the for-giveness exercises described in chapter 1. The process of forgiving a perfectionistic, critical, or distant parent, or another important person, may need to continue for many years, and for some spouses, for the rest of their lives. Spouses come to realize that is difficult, if not impossible, to maintain healthy confidence while harboring strong resentment toward another person.

I also encourage spouses to ask for forgiveness for all the ways in which their insecurity may have inflicted emotional harm on others. They may, for example, have been regularly overacting in anger because of some emotional hurt in the past.

After the use of forgiveness exercises, one often moves to the fourth stage of forgiveness, which is acceptance of hurts without in any way approving of them. This acceptance sometimes results in compassion for others. With acceptance can come empathy for others whose emotional hurts from childhood interfered with their ability to give in a loving, sensitive manner.

Marital Therapy

Both spouses must be involved in the healing process needed to bring about growth in confidence. Working on gratitude and overcoming perfectionistic thinking require a team effort. The spouses can coach each other to give thanks daily.

Marital therapy may be helpful when the struggle with insecurity is primarily the result of a spouse who is controlling, disrespectful, critical, emotionally distant, mistrustful, perfectionistic, or angry. Such spouses are asked to commit to working on overcoming their specific weaknesses in mature, self-giving marital love. And the insecure spouse is encouraged to correct the negative behavior of the other spouse.

Not infrequently, the negative behavior of the other spouse is the result of unresolved emotional pain from childhood or from modeling after a parent with the same psychological struggle. In that case, the pain needs to be uncovered and addressed through forgiveness.

To maintain their confidence, spouses need the friendship of their husbands or wives. When spouses are each other's best friends, they are there for each other, they encourage each other, they express gratitude for each other, and they cheer each other on through the difficulties of life. Strong marital friendship diminishes insecurity and anxiety. Scripture offers this praise of friendship:

> A faithful friend is a sturdy shelter:
>   he that has found one has found a treasure.
> There is nothing so precious as a faithful friend,
>   and no scales can measure his excellence.
> A faithful friend is an elixir of life;
>   and those who fear the Lord will find him.
>   (Sir 6:14–16)

The Role of Faith

Expressions of gratitude for God's love, protection, power, grandeur, and gifts are an essential aspect of Judeo-Christian worship, prayer, and meditation. Such spiritual exercises can lift people from their emotional pain and increase their confidence and hope in life.

Meditating on Scripture can also bring relief from insecurity and associated anxiety. Here are some examples of comforting passages from the Bible that can strengthen confidence.

> And this is the confidence which we have in him, that if we ask anything according to his will he hears us. (1 Jn 5:14)

I will trust, and will not be afraid;
for the LORD GOD is my strength and my song. (Is 12:2)

I can do all things in him who strengthens me. (Phil 4:13)

The Sacrament of Reconciliation is helpful for overcoming anger from past hurts, resolving the guilt that harms confidence, strengthening resolve against compulsive behaviors, and regaining the sense of oneself as a beloved child of God, which restores confidence. Saint John Paul II wrote that "the forgiven penitent is reconciled with himself in his inmost being, where he regains his own true identity."[6] Pope Benedict XVI also noted that true identity can be restored through reconciliation with God. "A man who is distant from God is also distant from himself, alienated from himself, and can only find himself by encountering God. In this way he will come back to himself, to his true self, to his true identity."[7] Both popes are saying that identities wounded by sin, ours and others', can be renewed in the loving embrace of God, which Catholics can experience in the sacraments.

Reflecting on the truth that spouses are sons and daughters of a loving God strengthens them against the temptation to measure themselves by the worldly standards of success—wealth and social status—which can diminish their self-worth. Saint John Paul II wrote that human perfection consists "in a dynamic relationship of faithful self-giving with others. It is in this faithful self-giving that a person finds a fullness of certainty and security."[8] In other

---

[6] John Paul II, Apostolic Exhortation *Reconciliation and Penance* (December 2, 1984), no. 31.

[7] Benedict XVI, General Audience (January 30, 2008).

[8] John Paul II, Encyclical Letter *Fides et ratio* (September 14, 1998), no. 32

words, Christ is our standard. If we measure ourselves in terms of becoming like him—while giving thanks for all the gifts and the grace God provides—we will have a firm foundation for our confidence.

Prudence Improves Communication

The family has the mission to guard, reveal and communicate love, and this is a living reflection of and a real sharing in God's love for humanity and the love of Christ the Lord for the Church His bride.

—Saint Pope John Paul II

Let your speech always be gracious.

—Colossians 4:6

The goal of this chapter is to assist spouses with loving and respectful communication, which is necessary for a healthy and happy marriage. Such communication produces a peaceful atmosphere in the home, reducing stress not only for the spouses but also for their children. The causes of communication conflicts and the harm they inflict are described, and the virtue of prudence is presented as an important habit for maintaining healthy communication.

Chad and Chloe

"I'm proud of all the hard work he does for me and the children," Chloe said of her husband, "but I wish Chad

John Paul II, Apostolic Exhortation on the Role of the Christian Family in the Modern World *Familiaris consortio* (November 22, 1981), no 17.

talked more to me. When he comes home, he just goes into a shell. Either he turns on the TV and watches sports all evening, or he sits in front of his tablet doing Lord knows what. Although I want to be with him in the evening, I can't stand watching sports and go to another room. When I try to talk to him, he doesn't even seem to hear me."

"What's your view on this?" I asked Chad.

He shrugged. "Maybe I really don't understand what's wrong."

I watched as anger flashed in Chloe's eyes. "See what I mean?" she said. "He never talks about anything!"

Chloe's parents enjoyed good communication and a close marital friendship. She yearned for the same type of closeness in her own marriage. Chad, in marked contrast, was raised in a home with significant conflict between his parents. He lacked good role models for marital communication, particularly in his father, who was quiet and rarely praised him. Without realizing it, Chad had brought significant communication weakness into his marriage.

Chad had a strong love for Chloe, and he thought it was evident by his working very hard to provide for her and their five children. He certainly did not view himself as an insensitive husband; yet Chloe felt lonely in the evenings because he did not seem to want to listen to her. She did not feel that her husband was the friend with whom she could share everything, and her disappointment was causing unhappiness in their marriage.

Benefits of Good Marital Communication

Although it could be argued that loving deeds are more important than sweet words, sharing joys, sorrows, worries, and successes with one's spouse is at the heart of a happy married life. Such communication is essential in maintaining and strengthening the friendship between husband and wife and in addressing the numerous challenges of family life.

The importance of respectful and patient listening and responding cannot be overstated. It protects spouses from loneliness—a powerful enemy of marital love—and its associated sadness, anxiety, insecurity, and anger. Good communication fosters a deeper marital friendship and enhances the oneness of husband and wife. It enables spouses to maintain their trust in each other and to keep their hearts open to each other. It is also a source of comfort and happiness for their children.

Healthy communication significantly diminishes the anxiety caused by bottling up worries and conflicts. The proverb "problems shared are halved" is true in a marriage in which husband and wife share their burdens with each other and solve difficulties together. It is doubly true when spouses also share their concerns with the Lord.

Damage from Poor Communication

In the absence of good marital communication, stress grows, trust decreases, walls arise, and loving feelings diminish. The result is loneliness, sadness, anger, anxiety, and weakened confidence. Spouses may seek to escape from this pain through compulsive behaviors involving media, shopping, sports, pornography, and drugs or alcohol. Alienated spouses are vulnerable to developing inappropriate relationships outside the marriage, which can lead to infidelity.

William Doherty, marriage and family scholar at the University of Minnesota, found a link between poor communication and marital breakdown. In his study of 886 Minnesotans who filed for divorce, 53 percent reported that not being able to talk with their spouses was a major contributing factor in their decision to divorce.[1]

Children need to see, through demonstrations of warmth, kindness, and courtesy, that their parents love each other. When considerate communication between parents is lacking, children develop sadness and anxiety. If excessive anger or controlling and disrespectful communication is frequent in their parents' marriage, children often fear that their parents will divorce.

Spouses' expressions of anger at each other in front of their children is a sign of their emotional immaturity and often selfishness. Rather than giving in to a destructive impulse, spouses need to refrain from communicating with each other until they can speak without anger, especially when children are present. Anger is best resolved through forgiveness. Chapter 1 describes the use of immediate forgiveness exercises that can protect the marriage and the children from the destructive effects of wrath. When anger is disproportionate, it can often be a sign of unresolved hurts from the past. These also can be resolved through forgiveness exercises.

Causes of Communication Difficulties in Marriage

Difficulties in marital communication can arise from numerous sources, of which spouses are often unaware, and include the following:

[1] Alan J. Hawkins, Brian J. Willoughby, and William J. Doherty, "Reasons for Divorce and Openness to Marital Reconciliation", *Journal of Divorce and Remarriage* 53, no. 6 (August 2012): 453–63.

- Failing to realize the importance of offering far more positive and cheerful comments than negative ones
- Losing awareness of the fundamental goodness in one's spouse
- Needing to control
- Being exhausted and irritable from the pressures of work and daily life
- Unrecognized fears of betrayal
- Feeling overly responsible and anxious
- Failing to set aside quality time for good communication
- Modeling after a parent's negative communication style
- Being fearful of one's spouse or parent
- Being emotionally distant
- Relying excessively on one's spouse to initiate communication and expressions of love (which occurs more often in husbands)
- Not wanting to hear about and to help carry the crosses of one's spouse or children
- Failing to forgive fully those who have harmed one or both spouses
- Lacking faith in God and failing to entrust marital stress to him.
- Not raising issues of mutual interest or importance in conversation
- Lacking gratitude for one's spouse
- Failing to place one's spouse before children, relatives, work, and hobbies
- Failing to master selfishness, excessive anger, anxiety, and controlling or emotionally distant behaviors

Let's now look at emotional conflicts that harm marital communication, many of which originate from unresolved hurts from the past.

Parental Modeling

Many weaknesses in marital communication are the direct result of modeling unconsciously after the communication style of a parent, most often the one of the same sex. It is not uncommon, however, to repeat the weaknesses of the parent of the opposite sex, especially if one has not forgiven that parent for past hurts and disappointments. Yet the more we forgive a parent for his weaknesses, the less likely we are to act and to communicate in the same way.

To identify the communication style of their parents, I ask spouses questions such as the following:

- Did your parents appear to enjoy talking with each other?
- Were they able to address major concerns without overreacting emotionally?
- Have you modeled after the communication style of one or both of your parents in some way?
- Has your spouse modeled after one or both parents?
- Even if you don't know for sure what your in-laws were like throughout their marriage, do you think your spouse grew up in a home with healthy marital communication?

Then I provide the following list and ask spouses to choose the words that describe the contrasting communication styles of their parents and in-laws.

loving	emotionally distant, cold
giving	selfish
actively listening	constantly talking or indifferent
courteous	critical
relaxed, trusting	anxious
respectful	controlling
cheerful	negative, sad

confident	insecure
gentle	harsh, arrogant
complimentary	critical
positive	negative
mature	dependent, childish
encouraging	unsupportive
forgiving	angry

The most common cause of communication problems for husbands is that they have copied the behavior of their emotionally distant or angry fathers. Wives, on the other hand, tend to mimic the disrespectful behavior of their controlling mothers or fathers. Spouses who had a controlling or angry parent of the opposite sex can sometimes repeat the same harmful communication pattern because they harbor a deep unconscious resentment toward that parent.

Pride is the major obstacle to admitting the weaknesses that a person has acquired by modeling after a parent. Yet being honest about these weaknesses and where they came from and discussing them openly with one's spouse will facilitate growth in self-knowledge, which is the first step in addressing communication problems.

Anger

A spouse who has not yet learned to master anger by growth in the virtue of forgiveness is likely to overreact to minor stresses with irritability and criticism. Yelling and rehashing past hurts are other expressions of anger; so is the passive-aggressive "silent treatment". The spouse who is at the receiving end of such anger can lose trust, put up walls, and become less communicative and loving over time.

Selfishness

Selfishness, the powerful enemy of marital love, manifests itself in an obsession with talking about oneself and one's feelings, unwillingness to listen, indifference to a spouse's needs, failure to include one's spouse in important decision-making, preoccupation with self-interests, and an inability to say "I am sorry" and ask for forgiveness.

Self-absorption leads to a reluctance to affirm or compliment, a preference for screen time rather than communication time with one's spouse and children, and an endless portrayal of oneself as a victim.

Need to Control

A controlling person tries to dominate conversation, fails to speak with respect, refuses to listen, interrupts regularly, tries to stop someone from expressing his views, and ends or changes conversations abruptly. A controlling person is also overly negative and prone to criticize his spouse in front of children, relatives, and even friends. Wives who had angry, addicted, or selfish fathers often feel the need to be in control. Husbands who had controlling mothers often manifest a controlling communication style.

Insecurity

An insecure person can be overly quiet, feel too inadequate to share ideas, or be overly critical and negative in an effort to enhance his self-esteem. Such people often speak too quickly, communicate in an anxious, immature manner, and rarely offer positive comments. Severely insecure people often have an overwhelmingly negative communication style with their spouses.

Sadness or Loneliness

People suffering from intense sadness or loneliness are often so consumed by emotional pain that they lack the energy for conversation. They can also be overly irritable and withdrawn. They give little emotional warmth and fail to respond in a positive, loving manner. Some lonely spouses, however, can be nonstop talkers because of their need for attention.

Anxiety

Anxious people often seem tense and irritable when speaking and are usually rather negative and critical. Conversation with such people is rarely relaxed. They can be overly independent and emotionally distant because of trust wounds from their childhood, marriages, or places of employment. Their excessive sense of responsibility coupled with an inability to detach from their activities can lead to overwork, causing more anxiety and irritability. They might then perceive their spouses and children as burdens rather than gifts.

The Virtue of Prudence in Resolving Communication Conflicts

There is every reason to hope that marital communication difficulties can be resolved if spouses are willing to grow in the knowledge of their weaknesses and the good habits, or virtues, that can overcome them. Prudence, in particular, can improve communication between spouses. "*Prudence* is the virtue that disposes practical reason to discern our true good in every circumstance and to choose the right means of achieving it" (*CCC* 1806). In other words, it is the ability to see what is to be done, or said, in a given situation. Growth in this virtue helps us to appreciate the observation of Pope Francis concerning marital communication. He said that living together is "an art" that involves three key phrases: "May I?", "Thank you", and "I'm sorry."[2] Knowing when these words are needed is the fruit of prudence.

Prudence and Vital Communication Issues

Let us consider the role prudence plays in three important aspects of good marital communication: (1) the style, or emotional tone, of the communication; (2) the content of the communication; and (3) the time spouses set aside for communication.

Communication Style

The communication style, or emotional tone, is as important as—and sometimes more important than—the content of a marital discussion. If words are not spoken in a loving and respectful manner, the spouse who hears them often becomes defensive and will not be able to receive what is communicated. Emotional tone, facial expression, and responsiveness are vital aspects of conversation and should reflect a deep love for one's spouse. When one focuses on being cheerful, trusting, and forgiving, one's facial expression and tone of voice are usually kind and loving.

Saint John Chrysostom's prudent advice for husbands on how to communicate with their wives contains timeless wisdom: "Whenever you give your wife advice, always begin by telling her how much you love her. Nothing will persuade her so well to admit the wisdom of your words as her assurance that you are speaking to her with sincere

---

[2] Francis, Address to Engaged Couples (February 14, 2014).

affection. Tell her ... that you love her more than gold."[3]
The same, of course, is true for wives offering advice to
their husbands.

Working on maintaining a loving and respectful communication style is demanding but immensely rewarding
for a marriage and for children. Past forgiveness exercises
for previous hurts from one's spouse or family of origin are
often part of the necessary work.

Content

Psychologist John Gottman, an expert in marital communication, has demonstrated that making positive comments is
essential to marital health. His recommendation that spouses
try to offer five positive comments for each negative one has
become the gold standard. Spouses, therefore, benefit from
monitoring the ratio of positive comments to negative ones
and then taking deliberate action to increase it.

Married couples should regularly discuss their emotional well-being. Discussing emotions is often easier for
wives than for husbands because they usually have been
talking about their feelings with their mothers, sisters, and
friends since childhood. Men, on the other hand, often
need encouragement from their wives to reveal their feelings. Catholic men whose fathers rarely discussed emotions have reported being helped by praying for greater
emotional awareness.

The differences in the emotional lives of men and
women enable spouses to complement each other. Because self-knowledge is the key to personal growth, a man
greatly benefits from a wife who can help him to become

---

[3] John Chrysostom, "Homily 20 on Ephesians 5:22–33", in *On Marriage and
Family Life*, trans. and ed. C. P. Roth and D. Anderson (Crestwood, N.Y.: St.
Vladimir's Seminary Press, 1986), 61.

more astute about his emotions, which are often the un-conscious causes of insensitive behaviors. By protecting and providing for their families, husbands can give their wives a sense of security that shields them from overreact-ing emotionally to problems that come along, particularly if they have not fully addressed hurts from the past. Also, a husband's rational and emotionally detached approach to solving problems is a tremendous asset to his wife and children, although the husband should respect his wife's intuition or emotional IQ, which is often higher than his. Strong feelings are often indicators that something must be done, but by themselves they do not spell out the right course of action. Prudence is needed for that.

A major source of marital stress is the failure to discuss problems—be they in the marriage, with the children or other family members, or at work. Problems need to be discussed in order for solutions to be found. Also, when spouses are sincerely trying to become other Christs to each other, they want to help each other carry their crosses by listening and offering supportive feedback.

When couples include the Lord in their discussions of difficult issues, through prayer, they usually become more aware that the Lord is with them, which increases their confidence and hope. In planning the size of their families, guiding the moral and spiritual development of their chil-dren, and other such challenging decisions, spouses need more than human wisdom. The awareness of the Lord's presence and support helps couples to discern his will for their lives and to address prudently the challenges of living as Christians in the world.

Time to Talk

Spouses can mistakenly assume that looking after their jobs, their children, and their home is enough to protect their marital friendship. They often spend so much of the day on their numerous responsibilities, followed by their personal interests or entertainments, that they put off communicating with each other until bedtime, when they are often too exhausted to engage in a beneficial discussion.

Deeds are a fundamental aspect of demonstrating one's love, but good communication is also vital. Thus, couples need to make time, every day if possible, for personal conversation. They need to make a daily conscious effort to say "thank you" for the gifts shared and the work done on behalf of the family. For their failings, they need to say "I am sorry." Spouses also need to discuss their needs, desires, and problems.

For conversation to be easier and something positive to look forward to, the home should be a safe haven from the world, where spouses feel free to express themselves openly and honestly. Sharing the evening meal, along with the rest of the family, is a great way to encourage conversation. Other activities that couples can do together, and with their children too, such as reading silently or aloud, playing or listening to music, watching or listening to an edifying program, and praying together, can ease the tensions of the day and begin fruitful conversations.

If possible, spouses should communicate several times during the day. For serious planning and problem solving, they should consider setting aside twenty minutes or more in the evening to talk alone. Parents of young children might need to wait until little ones are in bed, but they can usually tell older children that they need some privacy. In addition, taking time once a week to relax and to converse alone together outside the home, away from immediate responsibilities and pressures, is also beneficial. Such an activity could be as simple as taking a walk together.

Attentive Listening and Responding

Attentive listening and responding are key to good marital communication. The ability to listen respectfully is an essential aspect of receiving one's spouse, of self-surrender, and of successful transition from the self-absorbed "me" to the "we" of mature marital love.

Listening is vital to the process of self-surrender because it removes some of the obstacles to unity, such as our proud self-reliance and independent thinking. Listening helps us to recognize that we do not have all the answers and to appreciate more what others have to offer. Some spouses report that they listen better when they think, "My spouse wants only the best for me, the children, and others." Others report being helped by asking themselves, "What is the Lord saying to me now through my spouse?" Also helpful is Saint James' prudent advice that everyone "be quick to hear, slow to speak, slow to anger" (Jas 1:19).

A serious but common mistake that spouses make after listening attentively to their husbands or wives is failing to respond promptly. Silence can be perceived as indifference or a lack of respect, which can lead to sadness, anger, a loss of trust, and a decreased motivation to communicate. It is essential to affirm a spouse's verbal self-giving and encourage it. One should give a response right away, and it should reflect respect and love for the goodness of one's spouse, even though there may be some disagreement.

The response does not necessarily need to convey a solution to a problem. Sometimes one simply needs to be heard and to be reassured of the spouse's concern. That said, the listening spouse, especially one who is relying on God's wisdom to help the spouses as a couple, should pray for prudence, for the right words to say in the situation. A wife may express the view "All I want is for my husband to listen to me", but this demeans her husband's gifts and may reflect pride or selfishness. Caring spouses want to help each other find solutions to problems.

Unless there is truly a need for clarification, there is no need to restate what someone has just said. In fact, repeating to someone what he has just said can be experienced as both demeaning and controlling. Husbands and wives will know that they have been heard and understood based on their spouses' sympathetic and helpful responses.

Discussions, Not Arguments

We have need of prudence when we do not agree with our spouses. Our expressions of disagreement must be without anxiety, disrespect, or anger, especially in the presence of our children. If we feel angry about what we have heard, we should inwardly work on forgiving and not speak until our anger recedes. Apart from sounding the alarm in an emergency, we should not raise our voices toward our spouses or our children.

Angry feelings are normal in the face of wrongdoing, but we must learn not to use harsh words, which can escalate conflict and harm the people we love. "A soft answer turns away wrath, but a harsh word stirs up anger" (Prov 15:1). Prayer and meditation can help us to grow in prudence and self-control, which we need to say the right words at the right time. Catholics must take seriously the responsibility to grow in these virtues, for "if any one thinks he is religious, and does not bridle his tongue but deceives his heart, this man's religion is vain" (Jas 1:26).

When a person disagrees with his spouse, he needs to consider responding with refinement, as to someone with great goodness, someone who is a priceless gift. Many

Christian spouses report that when they pray before engaging in a serious, sensitive discussion, they have greater appreciation for each other and greater prudence and self-control. Praying together to the Holy Spirit for his sevenfold gifts is a good way to begin a weighty conversation.[4] So is praying the Rosary or the Chaplet of Divine Mercy.

With the help of prayer, couples find it easier to disagree respectfully with each other, saying things along these lines: "Dearest, thank you for relating your opinion. I respect it very much. My view of the situation differs from yours, however, and I would like to explain it." Then after explaining their points of view, spouses can end with: "I love you, and I know that we can come to an agreement."

No Secrets

When respect between spouses grows, so does trust. And the more spouses trust each other, the better they can give of themselves to each other. Complete self-giving excludes holding back anything and keeping secrets.

The deliberate withholding of important information from a spouse is a sign of serious mistrust, which will hurt the marriage if it is not addressed. Mistrust can arise from unresolved hurts in the marriage, in previous relationships, and in one's family of origin. These hurts need to be uncovered and healed through the power of forgiveness.

Expressing Needs

Many couples need to grow in the ability to identify and to express their needs to each other. We are not meant for

---

[4] The seven gifts of the Holy Spirit are wisdom, understanding, knowledge, fortitude, counsel, piety, and fear of the Lord.

radical independence, for pursuing happiness and taking care of ourselves all on our own. Rather, we are made to love and be loved in communion with others. We cannot love our spouses, however, if we do not know their needs. And since we cannot read their minds, they must tell us what their needs are.

Here is a list of needs that spouses often have difficulty expressing to each other. It can help to know that asking for these things in a respectful manner can build understanding and trust and can make a marriage stronger.

- More affection
- More positive, affirming, cheerful marital communication
- More real time together
- More romantic love
- One's spouse to listen more
- One's spouse to initiate affection and intimacy more
- One's spouse to make the marital friendship a higher priority
- One's spouse to work harder at mastering anger, selfishness, controlling behaviors, or emotionally distant behaviors

Correction of a Spouse

Couples often inadvertently harm themselves and their marriages by failing to address such serious difficulties as controlling, selfish, angry, or emotionally distant behaviors. The major reason for failing to talk about these things is the fear of upsetting one's spouse, but the failure to give correction to a husband or a wife who needs it is a failure to love that person enough to want what is best for him. Also, spouses cannot fulfill their vocation to become another Christ to each other without giving each other gentle, loving correction.

Communication about a spouse's weakness requires courage. Saint Paul's advice about giving correction is helpful: "Let the word of Christ dwell in you richly, as you teach and admonish one another in all wisdom" (Col 3:16). In other words, if spouses open themselves to the Word of God and let it renew their hearts and minds, they can have confidence about giving each other wise correction.

A prudent approach for correction in marriage is the sandwich technique. First, affirm your spouse's goodness. Then describe a weakness with an expression such as this: "Honey, I know you love me, and I love you, too, but at times you're being a bit [choose a weakness that needs correction: selfish, angry, insensitive, controlling, overly independent, or emotionally distant]." Then offer a suggestion for growth in a virtue that can help to replace the weakness. End the process by again praising your spouse's basic goodness and expressing confidence that he can make progress in this area with the help of grace.

Archbishop Fulton J. Sheen's observation about endurance in marriage has assisted many couples in seeking greater closeness through helping one another on the journey of personal growth:

> One of the greatest mistakes couples make is to think that their love will endure because it is strong. Rather, love continues not because of its strength but because it is related to the power of self-renewal. The love of a husband and wife is less a continuing thing than it is, like Calvary and the Resurrection, the finding of new life at a moment when it was believed that satiety was the master. In family life, two hearts do not move on a roadway

to a happier love; rather, every now and then they seem
on the brink of losing their love, only to find it on a
higher level.[5]

Archbishop Sheen is saying that true love grows in the face
of human weakness and failure. Couples need not fear that
their weaknesses will destroy their marriage if they commit themselves to supporting and encouraging each other
through positive communication *and* gentle correction.

Correction of Children

When couples practice the art of Christian correction with
each other, they find that correcting their children is easier. When children see the humility and the honesty of
their parents in accepting correction from each other, it is
easier for them to receive instruction too.

When everyone in the family, from the youngest to the
oldest, can accept that he is a work in progress, called to
grow more Christlike with each passing day, the pitfall
of shame and perfectionism, which can lead to harmful
obsessive-compulsive behaviors, can be avoided. Narcissism (extreme self-love), which has become an epidemic
among American youth, should be corrected. One of the
symptoms of narcissism is the inability to see one's faults
and to accept responsibility for them. The narcissist blames
others for his problems and mistakes and demands that others bend to his whims. He becomes angry when he cannot
have his way and treats parents, siblings, and others with a
lack of respect. In a family where faults are charitably called
out, such selfish behavior can be corrected and young

[5] Fulton Sheen, *Three to Get Married* (Princeton: Scepter, 1996), 154–55.

people can be trained to follow the Golden Rule—to treat others the way they would like to be treated.

The moral instruction of children is a weighty responsibility for parents, requiring courage and wisdom. But as Saint John Paul II explained, Catholic parents can have confidence in this task because they are given the graces they need for it through the Sacrament of Matrimony:

> For Christian parents the mission to educate, a mission rooted ... in their participation in God's creating activity, has a new specific source in the sacrament of marriage, which consecrates them for the strictly Christian education of their children: that is to say, it calls upon them to share in the very authority and love of God the Father and Christ the Shepherd, and in the motherly love of the Church, and it enriches them with wisdom, counsel, fortitude and all the other gifts of the Holy Spirit in order to help the children in their growth as human beings and as Christians.[6]

Faith and Communication

Catholic spouses report that setting aside time daily for communication with the Lord—in other words, for prayer—provides them with the comfort, the strength, and the wisdom they need to grow in virtue and to improve their relationships. Through prayer and participation in the sacraments, men and women become more like Christ. Attending Mass together every week has been shown to have numerous benefits for marriage and family life.

One of the most challenging weaknesses to overcome in communicating with others is a quick temper. In many

---

[6] John Paul II, Apostolic Exhortation on the Role of the Christian Family in the Modern World *Familiaris consortio* (November 22, 1981), no. 38.

cases, a spouse who becomes angry easily is repeating behavior learned in his family of origin. When this connection is uncovered, the spouse who is at the receiving end of anger should request that the abusive behavior stop. Both spouses will need to make frequent use of the Sacraments of Reconciliation and the Eucharist for the strength to overcome a bad habit and to forgive outbursts of anger, whether in the present or from the past.

In addition, some Catholic spouses report the benefits of weekly eucharistic adoration together and the daily Rosary. As spouses seek deeper union with the Lord together, they experience a stronger, more loving marital relationship.

9

Temperance Restrains Compulsions and Infidelity

The virtue of temperance guarantees every man mastery of the "lower self" by the "higher self".

—Saint John Paul II

God did not give us a spirit of timidity but a spirit of power and love and self-control.

— 2 Timothy 1:7

The goal of this chapter is to help spouses understand and master the powerful emotions and personality weaknesses that drive compulsive behaviors, including pornography use, that can lead to infidelity. It cannot be stated strongly enough that the use of pornography already betrays the marital trust by the virtual use of another person as a sexual object. Actual infidelity, however, creates the most severe betrayal pain felt in married life, and unless properly addressed, it can often result in marital separation and divorce.

This chapter uncovers the causes of infidelity, which in some marriages are present in both spouses, and identifies

John Paul II, General Audience (November 22, 1978), no. 3.

infidelity's extensive, long-term damage to spouses, children, and extended family. The virtue of temperance is presented as an important habit that can help overcome the numerous compulsive behaviors that can lead to infidelity and can help restrain reactions to the unfaithful spouse that can further damage the marriage.

Vince and Gwen

"I thought we had the ideal marriage," Gwen said. "Vince and I agreed about almost everything. When the children came along, we were a loving, happy Catholic family. We had a close marital relationship and went to Mass together every Sunday and sometimes during the week."

Then a bomb went off unexpectedly in their marriage: Gwen discovered that Vince, after using Internet pornography for several years, met a woman online and had an affair with her. Gwen was shocked by Vince's infidelity after thirty years of what she believed was a solid, happy marriage with two grown children. The trauma of his infidelity led to insomnia, depressive symptoms, loss of appetite and weight, and intense anger and rage in Gwen.

When Vince was asked if there was some serious marital or personal stress that had led him to be vulnerable to Internet pornography and infidelity, he was unable to identify any causes for his behaviors. He claimed that he loved Gwen very much and was sincerely repentant. He promised never to engage in these behaviors again. He thought and hoped that his statement of remorse would put the entire matter to rest. His communication style made it clear that he did not want to explore any deeper conflicts in his life. His explanation was very upsetting to Gwen and completely unacceptable to her. She knew something had to be seriously wrong and insisted that Vince work to identify it.

The uncovering process revealed that, after dinner, Vince stayed downstairs doing work on his laptop and watching television, while Gwen was upstairs in their bedroom with her iPad, reading magazines and novels. A growing loneliness developed in Vince, at a time when his career stress was more intense than ever. Unconsciously, he began seeking escape from his loneliness and shaken confidence by turning to Internet pornography. He developed a habit of seeking comfort from sex apart from his wife, making him vulnerable to infidelity. Vince recognized that his faith had weakened and that he had developed a more casual attitude toward sin. In fact, he had been denying the reality of sin in his life, resulting in a failure to examine his conscience and to confess his sins.

As Vince and Gwen grew in self-knowledge, they also recognized that they had become caught up in a preoccupation, if not an obsession, with material possessions and comfort-seeking behaviors. Succumbing to a materialistic mentality did not bring them happiness or fulfillment. Instead, it created an inner void, which left Vince further discouraged and prone to self-destructive impulses.

Compulsive Behaviors

Without realizing it, Vince and Gwen had gradually turned away from each other as they sought comfort, pleasure, and relief from stress through various compulsive behaviors. In the case of Gwen and Vince, these behaviors drove an unseen wedge between them that widened to the point of infidelity.

The most common compulsive behaviors in married couples include the following:

- Viewing Internet pornography
- Comfort-seeking eating, drinking, and video-gaming
- Excessive screen time
- Compulsive exercising and focusing on one's appearance
- Participating in many pleasurable activities without one's spouse
- Abusing alcohol or drugs
- Working inordinately
- Compulsive shopping
- Spending excessive time and energy on a best friend outside the marriage

These and other compulsive behaviors usually intensify over time; they are rarely overcome without a conscious effort to recognize them and to moderate them with the cultivation of temperance. They are often driven by unrecognized selfishness or an unconscious attempt to seek escape from stress. A person can come to depend on them to obtain a feeling of happiness or confidence, however fleeting. A compulsive behavior can become so dominant in a person's life that it meets the criteria for an addiction.[1] And once a person loses his self-control in one area, it is easy to lose it in another, including the temptation to commit adultery.

Warning Signs of Infidelity

A major warning sign of the risk of infidelity in a marriage is when a spouse places his interests or pleasure-seeking

---

[1] Sexual addiction, as in the case of pornography, however, is yet to be recognized in the latest psychiatric *Diagnostic and Statistical Manual of Psychiatric Disorders*.

compulsions above the good of the marriage and the family. The spouse on the brink of betrayal often withdraws from the romantic aspects of the marital relationship. He becomes emotionally aloof from the family and fails to maintain positive, cheerful communication not only with the other spouse but with the children.

Mood changes often occur in a disloyal spouse, such as increased irritability and anxiety. He begins to show signs of mistrust, insecurity, and guilt. Unfaithful spouses will often look unhappy because they are not psychologically capable of leading a double life.

Other telling behaviors, such as lying, secretiveness, financial irresponsibility, and absences from home, emerge. In addition, disloyal spouses will sometimes drop old friends and forge new relationships—for example, at the gym, among people who are having marital problems or are divorced. An important additional sign is obsessive and secretive use of the computer or the phone coupled with the refusal to give one's spouse the password of the device.

Infidelity often causes deep inner guilt over the betrayal of one's spouse, children, and God. The guilt is also driven by the unconscious knowledge that one has not worked hard enough on improving one's marriage and on trusting the Lord with the problems in his life. Guilt often produces inner sadness and excessive criticism of one's spouse to take the focus off one's own failure, "for he flatters himself in his own eyes that his iniquity cannot be found out and hated" (Ps 36:2). Guilty spouses are often unconsciously driven to make others feel as tormented as they are.

As Gwen reflected on Vince's behaviors over the previous two years, she recognized that there had indeed been subtle changes in his behavior and other warning signs that he was being unfaithful, but she had failed to identify them at the time.

Damage to Marital Love and Children

Even when falling short of being an addiction or a precursor of infidelity, many obsessions and compulsions are nevertheless harmful to individuals, their marriages, and their children. For example, an obsession with a career can injure one's spouse and children by causing a person to neglect the life balance necessary for a happy family life. Other damaging obsessions include preoccupations with material possessions or one's physical appearance, which can harden hearts toward family members. Compulsive comfort-seeking behaviors can make a person so self-absorbed that the needs of others go unnoticed.

The damage done by pornography has been well documented.[2] The porn user inhabits a fantasy world, with which his real life and relationships cannot compete. The use of pornography creates a distorted image of female or male beauty that harms the appreciation of the deep goodness and the true beauty of one's spouse. A porn-using spouse can become sexually frustrated and disappointed in marriage, because the other spouse fails to deliver the same thrills as porn does. Such dissatisfaction can lead to an increased vulnerability to marital infidelity.

Infidelity deeply damages a marriage. The betrayed spouse experiences loneliness, stress, insecurity, and anxiety. Anger, even rage, at the unfaithful spouse can become so intense that thoughts of revenge can emerge. Desperate vengeful behaviors, such as threatening phone calls to the spouse's lover, commonly accompany rage. For many betrayed wives and husbands, the most significant and lasting consequence of infidelity is the loss of trust in their

---

[2] A thorough treatment of the effects of pornography use can be found in Matt Fradd, *The Porn Myth* (San Francisco: Ignatius Press, 2017).

spouses. Many sincerely believe that they will never be able to recover the trust that was once present in the marriage.

Children also suffer from a lack of trust after they discover that one parent has been unfaithful to the other. In fact, they often fear that if they ever marry, they will be betrayed by their spouses, and they therefore often avoid marriage later in life. When youth discover that the parent of the same sex was unfaithful, they often feel deep disappointment because they no longer have a role model whom they can respect. When the infidelity is committed by the parent of the opposite sex, negative thinking about and fear of betrayal by the opposite sex can develop.

Damage to the Spiritual Life

Obsessions and compulsions can weaken a person's spiritual life because they are attempts at filling voids that God alone can fill. When they involve behaviors contrary to the moral law, they are sinful. In Catholic morality, there is a distinction between sinful actions that people do somewhat unthinkingly or out of habit and those that are consciously and deliberately chosen. The Church also makes a distinction between a serious matter, such as stealing another person's credit card, and a less serious matter, like stealing a pencil from one's employer. The more deliberate the action and the more serious the matter, the graver the sin, the greater the guilt, and the greater the damage to one's relationship with God.

But even small sins do spiritual harm. In fact, if one does not strive to overcome bad habits, they can grow worse and lead to grave sins. Blessed John Henry Cardinal Newman had keen insight into the relationship between bad habits and sin. He wrote:

Next we must consider the force of habit. Conscience at first warns us against sin; but if we disregard it, it soon ceases to upbraid us; and thus sins, once known, in time become secret sins. It seems then (and it is a startling reflection), that the more guilty we are, the less we know it; for the oftener we sin, the less we are distressed at it. I think many of us may, on reflection, recollect instances, in our experience of ourselves, of our gradually forgetting things to be wrong which once shocked us. Such is the force of habit.[3]

Given this wisdom, it is clear that Catholic couples must not allow themselves to become complacent about sinful compulsive behaviors.

Causes of Compulsive Behaviors

Uncovering the psychological causes of compulsive behaviors can help in overcoming them. The major causes are selfishness, weaknesses in confidence, loneliness, sadness, anger, and mistrust.

Selfishness

In my forty years of work with couples, selfishness has been the leading cause of marital infidelity. In fact, it should be the first thing considered when trying to understand any serious marital difficulty.

Selfishness fosters an obsession with one's happiness and a compulsive pursuit of pleasurable activities without considering how they could harm one's spouse or children. It is

---

[3] John Henry Newman, "Secret Faults", in *Parochial and Plain Sermons* (San Francisco: Ignatius Press, 1997), 37.

the major cause of materialism, pornography use, and substance abuse. A selfish person tends to see others as means to his own ends, such as the gratification of sexual desire. The selfish desire to use one's spouse as a sexual object is often the unspoken reason married couples use contraceptives. Whether couples realize it or not, habitual contraception makes sexual activity outside marriage easier.

The selfish spouse is not usually that way because of childhood or adult trauma. We often find, however, that selfish adults have made the pursuit of pleasure their primary goal in life, partly because during their youth their parents failed to correct their selfishness and to support their healthy character development, which is a form of emotional neglect. After lying dormant for decades, or at least after not being very noticeable, a person's selfishness can emerge in marriage, where the ability to love sacrificially is put to the test.

Weakness in Confidence

The next most frequent cause of compulsive behavior is a weakness in confidence and its associated anxiety and sadness. Work-related insecurities and stresses can create emotional tension that leads to an unconscious attempt to escape from it and to boost one's confidence through such things as sex outside marriage, whether virtual or real, and mood-altering substances. Husbands may be somewhat more vulnerable to struggles with insecurity because they often received less affirmation from their role models, their fathers, than wives received from their role models, their mothers. They also often receive little praise and affirmation in the competitive environments where they work.

Marital stress caused by a controlling, angry, selfish, negative, distant, unappreciative, or critical spouse can also seriously weaken the confidence of the other spouse and leave him vulnerable to seeking relief through compulsive behaviors that can lead to infidelity.

Loneliness and Sadness

Loneliness is another important cause of compulsive behaviors and infidelity. Loneliness can create a profound inner pain that, for some spouses, may even be stronger than physical pain. After understanding the nature and the influence of loneliness, many spouses have described it as a "killer".

The cause of loneliness and sadness in many spouses is unconscious family-of-origin loneliness due to their having lacked the comforting love of a father or a mother. These husbands and wives then incorrectly blame their spouses and become angry with them for the unhappiness in their marriages. Of course, some husbands and wives are indeed neglected by their spouses.

Anger

Strong anger is known to influence compulsive behaviors, as is mentioned in *Alcoholics Anonymous: The Story of How Many Thousands of Men and Women Have Recovered from Alcoholism* (more commonly known as *The Big Book*). Anger can arise from insensitive treatment by another person and can lead to a desire to strike back, in a passive-aggressive manner, through a variety of compulsive behaviors, including infidelity.

Earlier in life, anger is associated with sadness and anxiety, but later in life, it can be associated with a sense of pleasure in its expression. The great injustice that occurs is that this anger, meant for the person who has caused harm, is misdirected at one's spouse, sometimes through infidelity.

A person who had a controlling parent who treated him and the other parent with disrespect can falsely think that his spouse is like that controlling parent. Having never expressed anger toward or rebelled against this parent when young, a person can find unconscious pleasure in rebelling against a husband or wife through behaviors that cause the spouse pain.

Mistrust

The inability to trust and to feel safe with one's spouse as one's best friend makes a person vulnerable to insecurity, anxiety, and irritability. Unable to trust one's husband or wife, the anxious spouse can put up walls in the marriage and seek a trustworthy confidant elsewhere. Attempts to medicate away one's anxiety can lead to substance abuse and other compulsive behaviors.

Mistrust is a serious problem for spouses who have been traumatized by the divorce of their parents. The unconscious fear of being betrayed in loving relationships can lead to compulsive substance abuse beginning in adolescence, along with casual sex. Sadly, these behaviors increase the likelihood of being with untrustworthy people and becoming a disloyal spouse.

The Virtue of Temperance

Growing in the virtue of temperance can be of great value in addressing compulsive behaviors, preventing unfaithfulness, and healing the wounds caused by marital infidelity. "*Temperance* is the moral virtue that moderates the attraction of pleasures and provides balance in the use of created goods. It ensures the will's mastery over instincts and keeps desires within the limits of what is honorable. The temperate person directs the sensitive appetites toward what is good and maintains a healthy discretion" (*CCC* 1809).

Pope John Paul II understood that the virtue of temperance is the key to self-mastery:

> A temperate man is one who is master of himself. One in whom passions do not prevail over reason, will, and even the "heart". A man who can control himself! If this is so, we can easily realize what a fundamental and radical value the virtue of temperance has. It is even indispensable, in order that man may be fully a man. It is enough to look at some one who, carried away by his passions, becomes a "victim" of them—renouncing of his own accord the use of reason (such as, for example, an alcoholic, a drug addict)—to see clearly that "to be a man" means respecting one's own dignity, and therefore, among other things, letting oneself be guided by the virtue of temperance.[4]

Many unfaithful spouses come to understand that their infidelity was related to a surrender to selfishness and excessive comfort-seeking behaviors, which gradually took over their lives without their being fully aware of the damage being done to them and to their spouses. They truly became slaves to a compulsion, as Saint Paul described his own condition: "I can will what is right, but I cannot do it. For I do not do the good I want, but the evil I do not want is what I do" (Rom 7:18–19).

Temperance for Self-Mastery

Self-denial and self-control are aspects of temperance. Regular practice of *self-denial*, which the Church asks of Catholics on Fridays and during the penitential season of Lent,

[4]John Paul II, General Audience (November 22, 1978), no. 3.

helps Catholics to gain mastery over their appetites. *Self-control* is restraining one's impulses in order to behave in a responsible, loving, mature fashion.

The benefits of self-control were seen clearly in a study by Duke University that followed 1,037 persons from childhood to age thirty-two.[5] Those who could better regulate their impulses were four times less likely to have a criminal record, three times less likely to be addicted to drugs, and half as likely to become single parents.

Many spouses in modern Western societies lead comfortable lives and rarely think of their need for the virtue of temperance. Instead, they unconsciously pursue lifestyles that will provide them with as much comfort and pleasure as possible. And yet, as Pope John Paul II pointed out, temperance is needed if for no other reason than to maintain our physical health:

> In this connection, the statistics and files of hospitals all over the world, could say a great deal. Also doctors who work on the advisory bureaus to which married couples, fiancés and young people apply, have great experience of this. It is true that we cannot judge virtue on the exclusive basis of the criterion of psychophysical health; there are many proofs, however, that the lack of the virtue, of temperance, sobriety, damages health.[6]

Temperance and the Discovery of Infidelity

Catholic marriage is a both a covenant and a contract. Catholic spouses promise to stick together through thick and

[5] T. E. Moffitt et al., "A Gradient of Childhood Self-Control Predicts Health, Wealth, and Public Safety", *Proceedings of the National Academy of Sciences* 108, no. 7 (February 2011): 2693–98, https://doi.org/10.1073/pnas.1010076108.

[6] John Paul II, General Audience (November 22,1978), no. 5.

thin until death, and this promise is not voided when one of the spouses commits adultery. The virtue of temperance not only helps to check destructive compulsive behaviors and to prevent infidelity but also helps spouses to avoid making the following mistakes after infidelity has been discovered:

- Insistence upon an immediate separation
- Failure to see the goodness in the offending spouse
- Informing children and relatives immediately
- Refusal to identify and to address the emotional or character weaknesses of both spouses
- Blaming one's spouse exclusively for the infidelity
- Refusing to try to understand and to forgive
- Assuming the victim role to justify constant angry and disrespectful communication
- Fear of correcting the offending spouse
- Failure to obtain advice and support from those loyal to marriage
- Expecting the offended spouse to "get over it" quickly
- Lack of understanding as to how difficult it is to heal the infidelity-mistrust wound
- Failure to recognize that faith is essential in reestablishing trust and in resolving anger

Temperance and Forgiveness for Mastering Anger

For understandable reasons, most offended spouses have great difficulty in controlling their anger with unfaithful spouses. An offended spouse is encouraged to identify the causes of the infidelity and to work on forgiving the offender in order to protect his own psychological and spiritual health and to save the marriage. Some of the following prayers are helpful for controlling anger:

> Lord, forgive him; he did not know what he was really doing.
>
> I am powerless over my anger and want to turn it over to you, God.
>
> Lord, take my sadness and my anger.
>
> I hate the other person and want to punish him. Lord, free me from my rage.

These prayers are particularly helpful if the victim spouse has not only uncontrollable anger but also impulses for revenge. Anger over infidelity can also decrease through the graces of the Sacrament of Reconciliation.

The decision to temper one's anger by not expressing it as passionately or as often as one would like and to work on understanding and forgiving the unfaithful spouse diminishes not only anger but also the associated sadness, anxiety, and mistrust caused by infidelity. Yet forgiveness of such a betrayal is not easy. Among the obstacles to forgiveness are the following:

- Failure to understand that anger blocks healing and can make one a prisoner of one's past
- Belief that the hurt is so great that forgiveness is not possible
- Use of anger to keep the spouse at a distance and to protect oneself from further hurt
- Feeling of pleasure and revenge in expressing anger and rage
- Desire to punish the unfaithful spouse
- Family-of-origin weakness in trust

- Difficulty in seeing and being loyal to the goodness in the unfaithful spouse
- Lack of change in the behavior of the unfaithful spouse
- Abortion trauma in the past
- Weakness of faith in the power of God's mercy
- Guilt and denial regarding how one may have contributed unconsciously to marital stress
- Desire to harm the spouse's relationship with the children

Besides opening both spouses to the power of forgiveness, restraining anger has other benefits. It helps both spouses to stop blaming each other and to commit themselves to healing the marriage. As both spouses admit and take ownership for the ways they have harmed their relationship, understanding, compassion, and mercy grow. Tenderness, affection, and even trust can then be restored.

Temperance for Mastery of Fear and Rebuilding Trust

When an adulterer is sincerely repentant and is discussing and working on resolving the issues that led to the infidelity, the other spouse has a responsibility to God, the marriage, and the children to enter one of the most difficult psychological and spiritual journeys—rebuilding trust and allowing oneself to become vulnerable again. As difficult as this can be, its benefits are numerous, as described in chapter 5.

After infidelity, many injured spouses think that they will never be able to trust again. While understanding, forgiving, and working on the causes of the infidelity slowly rebuild trust, fear of further betrayal often continues to arise and to threaten the healing process. Catholic spouses report the benefit of prayer in overcoming fear; for example: "Lord, I trust you with our marriage. Help me to trust and to feel safe with my spouse again." Here is another meditation, which was shared by a spouse overcoming infidelity trauma: "Lord, I trust you today with our marriage. Help me to trust my spouse more each day."

Growth in trust has to be associated with resolving betrayal anger through a forgiveness process. Failure to do so results in unconscious or conscious anger encapsulating fears and sadness. The failure to work on forgiveness is a leading reason for the inability to rebuild marital trust.

Gratitude for the goodness in one's spouse, which is still present even after the sin of adultery, is also essential in rebuilding marital trust and love. It can be helpful for the injured spouse to write down all the good qualities in the other spouse. Such an exercise can counter the falsehood that infidelity has destroyed them.

Temperance for Mastery over Guilt

Guilt is an appropriate response to committing the sin of adultery. Guilt is extreme, however, if the adulterer, after confessing his sin and asking forgiveness, obsesses over the wrong done and refuses to believe it can be forgiven by God and by his spouse. This falsehood, a cognitive distortion, can result in severe depression and even suicidal thoughts. Effective help here is repeated recourse to the Sacrament of Reconciliation, which usually leads to significant emotional and psychological relief. At times, psychotherapy may be needed to overcome perfectionistic thinking and low self-esteem, both of which might have contributed to the adultery in the first place and therefore make it difficult to accept God's forgiveness.

On the other hand, an offending spouse may downplay the harm caused by his infidelity. This may be the influence of a sex-obsessed culture filled with rationalizations for extramarital sex and steeped in pornography. The intervention of a Catholic counselor, a family member, or a trusted member of the clergy might be needed to help the unfaithful husband or wife to admit the seriousness of adultery.

The Role of Faith

Faith in God's love and mercy helps couples to see the truth about their actions in the light of Christ. The *Catechism* presents clear teaching on marital infidelity that can strengthen spouses with its liberating truth: infidelity is both a form of idolatry and an injustice:

> When two partners, of whom at least one is married to another party, have sexual relations—even transient ones—they commit adultery. Christ condemns even adultery of mere desire (cf. Mt 5:27–28). The sixth commandment and the New Testament forbid adultery absolutely (cf. Mt 5:32; 19:6; Mk 10:11; 1 Cor 6:9–10). The prophets denounce the gravity of adultery; they see it as an image of the sin of idolatry (cf. Hos 2:7; Jer 5:7; 13:27).
>
> Adultery is an injustice. He who commits adultery fails in his commitment. He does injury to the sign of the covenant which the marriage bond is, transgresses the rights of the other spouse, and undermines the institution of marriage by breaking the contract on which it is based. He compromises the good of human generation and the welfare of the children who need their parents' stable union. (2380–81).

Faith also helps couples to trust in the saving power of God to free them from being emotional prisoners to their past, their compulsive behaviors, and their sexual temptations. After the origins of the infidelity are uncovered and addressed, Catholic couples can turn them over to God through prayer and frequent reception of the sacraments, confident that the Lord of love will guide them toward greater freedom through growth in the virtue of temperance.

10

Justice Prevents Divorce

Being rooted in the personal and total self-giving of the couple, and being required by the good of the children, the indissolubility of marriage finds its ultimate truth in the plan that God has manifested in His revelation.

—Saint John Paul II

Have you not read that he who made them from the beginning made them male and female, and said, "For this reason a man shall leave his father and mother and be joined to his wife, and the two shall become one"? So they are no longer two but one. What therefore God has joined together, let no man put asunder.

—Matthew 19:4–6

The Church certainly knows the power of psychological conflicts and sin at work in individuals and in societies, which at times almost leads one to despair of the goodness in a particular marriage. But through her faith in Jesus, crucified and risen, the Church is even more conscious of the power of forgiveness and self-giving love, in spite of any injury or injustice.

John Paul II, Apostolic Exhortation on the Role of the Christian Family in the Modern World *Familiaris consortio* (November 22, 1981), no 20.

The goal of this chapter is to help couples understand that most serious marital conflicts can be resolved and divorce thereby prevented. The myths about divorce, as well as its origins and the severe harm it inflicts on innocent spouses and children are presented. The virtue of justice is described as a major factor in preventing divorce and protecting children and society.

The Divorce Announcement

Spouses are often shocked by the announcement that divorce proceedings have been initiated by the person to whom they have been happily married. The words conveyed by such an announcement are usually along these lines: "I am deeply unhappy in our marriage and believe we should go our separate ways. The children will be fine. They will be happy if we are happy. I hope that you'll be supportive of my decision to divorce and be sensitive to our children as each of us enters a new phase of our lives." This announcement is especially shocking when the spouse receiving it is unaware of serious problems in the marriage such as infidelity, constant arguing, or severe financial stress.

The spouse initiating the breakup is usually determined to divorce and often refuses to participate in marital counseling or in any Church-related programs to help troubled marriages. If, however, the spouse agrees to counseling at the request of children, relatives, or a close friend who loves the family, unresolved hurts from the past are often uncovered. In such cases, the underlying causes of sadness or anger can be resolved, and the unhappy spouse can be persuaded to reconsider divorce and to engage in the hard work of healing. Then trust can grow and love can be rediscovered.

In this chapter, we will examine successful approaches to preventing divorce. The good news is that emotional wounds and personality weaknesses can be uncovered and resolved in most marriages. The spiritual life is essential in the healing process. Given the unique personalities and backgrounds of each spouse, two becoming one without the Lord is a difficult goal to obtain. It requires a daily commitment to growth in good habits with the help of grace.

Giving Up Too Quickly

It is clear from the research on divorce that many couples give up too quickly on their marriage. In a national survey of divorced men and women conducted by the University of Texas at Austin, only about one-third said that they and their ex-spouses had worked hard enough to stay together. The most frequently cited reason for their lack effort was a lack of commitment to the marriage.[1] The failure to remain committed to a spouse and to the hard work necessary to keep a marriage strong is partly the fault of family members, friends, mental health professionals, and sometimes even clergy who do not do enough to support the Sacrament of Matrimony. Other important reasons why couples quit too quickly are a lack of confidence that their problems can be overcome and a denial of the severe harm that divorce causes to spouses, their children and other relatives, and society at large.

There are a number of myths about marriage and divorce, including the following, that are widely promoted and believed:

[1] Norval Glenn, foreword to *Between Two Worlds: The Inner Lives of the Children of Divorce*, by Elizabeth Marquardt (New York: Three Rivers Press, 2006), xxii.

- Divorce will not harm the children, my spouse, or me.
- Divorce is the only solution to my unhappiness.
- What is good for me is good for my children.
- I can still be an excellent parent even though I divorce.
- Our marital conflicts cannot be resolved.
- My childhood and family background are not related to my marital unhappiness.
- My marital unhappiness is entirely caused by my spouse.
- Love cannot be rediscovered, nor can trust be restored.
- Good divorces are better for children than unhappy marriages.
- I will be much happier if I divorce.
- I am entitled to an annulment in the Catholic Church.

Have we not heard these before? They are so widespread in our society that they are held to be undeniable truths. As a result, couples lose hope in their marriages all too easily.

The Benefits of Divorce Are "Oversold"

Dr. Linda Waite of the University of Chicago has debunked the myth that divorce is a solution to unhappiness. In her research, she found that among people who rated their marriages as "very unhappy", 80 percent of those who stuck it out reported themselves as happily married five years later. Those spouses who separated were, on average, no happier than those who stayed married. Spouses who divorced and remarried were also no happier than those who stayed married.[2] Thus, Waite concluded, "The benefits of divorce have been oversold."[3]

The reason divorce often fails to deliver happiness, Waite found, is that marriage is often not the source of unhappiness. Unhappy marriages are less common than unhappy spouses, she discovered: three out of four unhappily married adults are married to someone who is happy with the marriage. If a person's unhappiness lies in himself and not in the marriage, divorce is unlikely to make him any happier.

Research shows that divorce rates are higher in second marriages than in first marriages. This higher failure rate may be due to the fact that the unhappy person is still unhappy, even after divorce and remarriage. In fact, he could be even unhappier than before, given the severe damage to his ability to trust and to commit that the divorce might have caused.

Divorce Ambivalence

Research at Penn State confirmed that more than two-thirds of divorces involving couples with children do not involve highly conflicted marriages.[4] In fact, most spouses who are considering divorce have highly ambivalent thoughts and feelings. Deep within their hearts, Catholic spouses still recognize the beauty and the holiness of marriage, the goodness in their spouses, and the benefits of marriage for

[2] Linda Waite and Maggie Gallagher, *The Case for Marriage: Why Married People Are Happier, Healthier, and Better Off Financially* (New York: Doubleday, 2000), 148.

[3] Ibid.

[4] Paul R. Amato and Alan Booth, *Generation at Risk: Growing Up in an Era of Family Upheaval* (Cambridge, Mass.: Harvard University Press, 1997), 220.

their children. Research involving 2,500 divorcing people revealed that spouses are a lot more ambivalent about divorce and more reluctant to divorce than has been realized. About one in four parents thought their marriages could still be saved, and in about one in four couples, both spouses thought so too. Three in ten individual spouses indicated potential interest in reconciliation services, as did both spouses in three out of ten couples.[5]

Given that many of those seeking divorce are not in highly conflicted marriages and have mixed feelings about the direction they are taking, it can be safely assumed that if more people encouraged fragile marriages, there might be fewer divorces as a result. Given the harm divorce does to everyone involved, especially children, more should be done to prevent it.

Harm to Children

Working with children traumatized by their parents' divorce is one of the most stressful and emotionally upsetting aspects of my professional life. These children often look as if they have been in the middle of a battlefield, where they have been severely wounded by fears, sadness, confusion, profound insecurity, and intense betrayal anger, which is usually denied, especially by sons concerning their fathers. Many youths may even struggle with significant guilt, believing that they bear responsibility for the divorce.

A number of studies demonstrate that, from a child's perspective, there is no such thing as a good divorce. In

---

[5] William J. Doherty, Brian J. Willoughby, and Bruce Peterson, "Interest in Marital Reconciliation among Divorcing Parents", *Family Court Review* 49, no. 2 (April 2001): 313–21.

one study, the late family scholar Norval Glenn found that children whose parents had a "good divorce" fared worse than those whose parents had unhappy marriages.[6] He also found that the negative effects of divorce on children cannot be avoided merely by parents being cooperative. Even in best-case scenarios, in the wake of their parents' divorce, children are likely to experience a family move, marked declines in their family income, a stressed-out single mother, and substantial periods of paternal absence— all factors that put them at risk.

In an important book on the children of divorce, *Torn Asunder*, from the proceedings of a conference held at the John Paul II Institute for Studies in Marriage and Family at the Catholic University of America, many family scholars, some of whom are adult children of divorce, present findings on the psychological and spiritual harm to youth and adults caused by divorce.

The harm done to children follows them into adulthood. Young adults from divorced families regularly struggle with fear of abandonment, mistrust, insecurity, anger, sadness, and a fear of marriage, which has contributed to the retreat from marriage and the extraordinary explosion of cohabitation in America. This has contributed to declining Catholic marriage rates. There were 426,309 Catholic marriages in 1969; 261,626 in 1999; 154,450 in 2014; and 144,148 in 2016.[7] According to Dr. Bradford Wilcox,

> From 1960 to 2007, the percentage of American women who were married fell from 66% to 51%, and the percentage of men who were married fell from 69% to 55%.

[6] Norval Glenn, "How Good for Children Is the Good Divorce?", *Propositions* 7 (April 2012): 1–7.

[7] The Center for Applied Research in the Apostolate, https://cara.george town.edu/frequently-requested-church-statistics.

Yet at the same time, the number of cohabiting couples increased fourteen-fold—from 439,000 to more than 6.4 million. Because of these increases in cohabitation, about 40% of American children will spend some time in a cohabiting union.[8]

Divorce contributes not only to avoidance of marriage and to cohabitation but also to more divorce. Adults whose parents divorced are 89 percent more likely to divorce, compared with adults who were raised in intact families. Children of divorce who marry other children of divorce have an even higher risk of ending up divorced.[9]

The proportion of emotionally troubled adults is about three times greater among adults whose parents divorced than among adults from intact families, and adult children of divorce are more vulnerable to suicidal thinking and behavior. A 2011 study demonstrated the suicide risk in those whose parents divorced before they were eighteen: men from divorced families have more than three times the risk of suicidal thinking than men whose parents did not divorce.[10]

Harm to Spouses

After a divorce, mothers often end up with custody of their children. Many report being overwhelmed by the

[8] W. Bradford Wilcox, "The Evolution of Divorce", *National Affairs* 37 (Fall 2018), https://www.nationalaffairs.com/publications/detail/the-evolution -of-divorce.

[9] Nicholas H. Wolfinger, *Understanding the Divorce Cycle: The Children of Divorce in Their Own Marriages* (New York: Cambridge University Press, 2005), 74.

[10] E. Fuller-Thomson and A. D. Dalton, "Suicidal Ideation among Individuals Whose Parents Have Divorced: Findings from Representative Canadian Community Survey", *Psychiatry Research* 187, no. 1–2 (May 2011): 150–55, http://doi.org/10.1016/j.psychres.2010.12.004.

burden of raising children without the father in the home, even in cases in which the father remains involved. Former wives also often experience the pain of severe loneliness. This stress can lead to mistrust and withdrawal from children, emotional overreactions in sadness and in anger, substance abuse, and cohabitation with untrustworthy men. Self-mastery over anger with an ex-spouse is extremely challenging and difficult.

Given that roughly two-thirds of divorce proceedings are initiated by women in marriages with low levels of conflict, men are more likely than women to be divorced against their will.[11] The great majority of divorced men lose regular day-to-day contact with their children. Many find this patently unfair to fathers, particularly those who were divorced unwillingly and who were not guilty of serious wrongdoing. These men often develop intense loneliness and profound sadness that can lead to depressive illness, weaknesses in confidence, mistrust, and anger. They typically lose their homes and a substantial share of their monthly income. The emotional pain experienced by these men can interfere with their ability to meet the demands of daily life.

Harm to the Extended Family

Everyone related to a divorced couple suffers from the divorce. Former in-laws regularly experience a profound sadness over the loss of someone they loved as a son, daughter, brother, or sister as the result of a divorce. Parents and siblings of a divorced adult are saddened by the suffering the person experiences during and after the

---

[11] W. Bradford Wilcox, "The Evolution of Divorce", *National Affairs* 38 (Winter 2019):87.

divorce. Nieces and nephews can also be affected and can develop significant sadness and fear of making a commitment to marriage.

Relationships between the children of the divorced couple and grandparents, aunts, and uncles change, often for the worse. Some grandparents are denied all contact with their grandchildren. Loving grandparents who remain close can still be saddened by the severe emotional pain that their grandchildren suffer.

The intense pain experienced by the extended family is one of the many reasons family members should request that spouses work on healing their marriage for at least two years before going through with a divorce. Also, family members should not hold back from questioning or possibly criticizing those who support divorce, whether they are friends, relatives, marital therapists, or even clergy.

Harm to Friendships

Married couples often experience both a deep sadness and a sense of loss when friends divorce, especially those in low-conflict marriages. They often become fearful about the stability and the future of their own marriages. They also experience increased stress in response to their children's fears and catastrophic thinking that their parents' marriages might end in divorce.

To protect themselves from these fears and stresses, married couples often drift away from friends who are divorced, leaving the divorced spouses even lonelier and more isolated. When couples seek a divorce, they need to be encouraged to look at all the traumatic changes it will cause in their lives, including the loss of good friends.

Factors That Contribute to Divorce and the Divorce Mentality

To avoid divorce and all the harm it causes, it is important to understand and to address the factors that contribute to it. In our experience, there is rarely a marriage problem that cannot be overcome.

Communication Conflicts

A 2012 study of 886 Minnesotans who filed for divorce demonstrated the importance of good marital communication. Fifty-three percent identified not being able to talk together as one of the major contributing factors to the decision to divorce.[12] Through counseling or classes, spouses can learn to improve their methods of communication. If there is an unresolved hurt blocking positive communication, that can be addressed through growth in forgiveness and trust.

Selfishness

The next most common cause for seeking divorce is selfishness, the powerful enemy of marital love. Selfish ambition in one's career, physical appearance, or social life can result in seeking happiness primarily outside the family. These issues can become obsessions, resulting in a deep unhappiness and a decision to leave one's spouse.

Spouses who give in to selfishness often fail to experience the fulfillment they have been seeking, and they mistakenly blame their marriages. They need to be

---

[12] Alan J. Hawkins, Brian J. Willoughby, and William J. Doherty, "Reasons for Divorce and Openness to Marital Reconciliation", *Journal of Divorce and Remarriage* 53, no. 6 (August 2012): 453–63.

encouraged to believe that true joy can be found in total self-giving.

Lack of Insight about the Real Causes of Unhappiness

Spouses who have given in to selfishness are not the only ones who can be unaware of the real causes of their unhappiness. Spouses in low-conflict marriages who seek divorce for any reason often deny that they have unresolved hurts from the past and character flaws that first emerged when they were young. Instead, they blame their spouses exclusively for their unhappiness.

To resolve marriage problems and to avoid divorce, spouses need to grow in self-knowledge about their primary weaknesses and their unresolved hurts from their families of origin or past relationships, especially unresolved sadness or anger with a parent.

Loneliness and Sadness

Among highly sensitive women, a common reason for considering divorce is the intense pain of loneliness. This loneliness can arise from unresolved sadness with one or both parents in childhood, from previous relationships, or from the marriage. Spouses whose parents divorced or were addicted may also struggle with intense inner sadness and loneliness that is often unrecognized. The most common type of loneliness we see in spouses who consider divorce stems from the father relationship or is caused by having an emotionally distant spouse.

In such cases, both spouses have work to do—to uncover the current and past causes of sadness and loneliness and to reveal the reasons one of the spouses is emotionally distant, unavailable, or otherwise unable to maintain a friendship with the other spouse.

Unresolved Anger

Anger expressed in words or actions, either actively or passively, damages relationships. Repeated expressions of anger can break down trust and love between spouses. Unresolved anger in a spouse is sometimes the result of being hurt by a parent. Without realizing it, one can misdirect this anger at one's spouse. Regardless of its cause, unchecked growth of anger or of resentment toward an angry spouse can cover earlier feelings of warmth and tenderness and can lead to a mistaken belief that one can never love one's spouse again.

The best antidote to anger is forgiveness, as explained in chapter 1. If one is angry at a parent for failures in the past, he needs to forgive that parent in order not to misdirect anger at others. An angry person must regularly ask forgiveness of those he has hurt by wrathful words or deeds. Those hurt by the anger of their spouses must learn to forgive this weakness. The balm of forgiveness helps everyone to grow in the needed virtues of gentleness and self-control.

Mistrust

Another problem that leads spouses to consider divorce is a weakness in trusting or in feeling safe. Mistrust interferes with giving and receiving love. The fact is, most spouses enter marriage with some trust weakness from one of their parents or from others that can emerge under stress. When it does, it can become a major factor in the development of marital unhappiness. It is simply not possible to be happy in marriage unless spouses trust enough to give themselves completely to each other. Fear blocks the fulfillment found in moving from "me" to "we".

Mistrust can have deep roots in early childhood experiences. These need to be uncovered and addressed in order for spouses to have the intimacy needed in marriage, as described in chapter 5.

Insecurity

A lack of self-confidence, beginning in childhood or early adulthood, can lead to many problems in marriage, such as addiction and infidelity, that, if unresolved, can lead to divorce. Often insecurity stems from having a father who never built up his child's confidence. Every child wants to please his father and gain his acceptance, which fuels the confidence essential to maintaining a healthy personality.

Confidence weakness can emerge after many years of a happy marriage, when a spouse's love is no longer strong enough to control the weaknesses brought into the marriage. Unconsciously, a spouse can seek romantic involvement outside the marriage in an attempt to enhance self-esteem and to decrease anxiety and sadness. A small percentage of spouses will turn to those of the same sex to escape from pain that originated with rejection by the parent or peers of that sex.

All spouses who consider divorcing for the sake of an extramarital relationship should look closely at their childhood relationships with each parent to determine whether they entered their marriage with a confidence deficit.

Controlling Behaviors

People who are controlling seriously harm others by failing to treat them with respect. Spouses who are subjected to disrespectful controlling behaviors for many years become depressed about their marriage and often consider separation or divorce. A person traumatized by a controlling husband or wife can become vulnerable to individuals of the opposite sex who are emotionally sensitive and kind.

As noted in chapter 3, controlling behaviors often result from not feeling safe in childhood due to parents who struggled with substance abuse, excessive anger, controlling behaviors, or selfishness. The other major cause of controlling behavior is modeling after a controlling parent.

Unfortunately, many people who consider divorcing a controlling spouse have never asked to be treated more respectfully. All too often, controlling spouses are not very aware of how disrespectful and hurtful their behavior is. To prevent divorce, both spouses need to identify the harmful behavior and its origins. Through willingness to communicate and to show respect, spouses can save their marriages.

Lack of Knowledge Regarding the Truth about Marriage

Over the past fifty years, many Catholic couples have entered marriage without a deep understanding of the beautiful call to holiness in the Sacrament of Matrimony. The Catholic Church is the only institution in the world that continues to defend the indissolubility of marriage—to say that marriage vows last until death. When Jesus taught this to his apostles, they were shocked at the difficulty of this teaching, saying, "It is not expedient to marry" (Mt 19:10).

The apostles did not yet understand what Christ would reveal through his death and Resurrection, through the coming of the Holy Spirit, and through the sacraments of the Church, including Matrimony: that Christ would share his very life with us so that we can love as he does. The Church understands very well that "without his help man and woman cannot achieve the union of their lives for which God created them 'in the beginning'" (*CCC* 1608).

Many Catholics are unaware that their marriage in the Church is more than a civil contract, which can be broken at will; it is a covenant of lifelong love such that "their belonging to each other is the real representation, by means of the sacramental sign, of the very relationship of Christ with the Church."[13] This is a high calling indeed, and when a marriage is put to the test, spouses can be inspired by the realization that if they persevere in their mission with the help of God's grace, the greatest love can emerge.

Many Catholics are equally unaware that divorce is gravely immoral. According to the *Catechism*:

> *Divorce* is a grave offense against the natural law. It claims to break the contract, to which the spouses freely consented, to live with each other till death. Divorce does injury to the covenant of salvation, of which sacramental marriage is the sign. Contracting a new union, even if it is recognized by civil law, adds to the gravity of the rupture: the remarried spouse is then in a situation of public and permanent adultery....
>
> Divorce is immoral also because it introduces disorder into the family and into society. This disorder brings grave harm to the deserted spouse, to children traumatized by the separation of their parents and often torn between them, and because of its contagious effect which makes it truly a plague on society. (2384–85)

The Psychological View of Marriage

As noted earlier, in the modern psychological approach to marriage, one's primary obligation is not to one's family but to oneself; hence, marital success is defined not by meeting obligations to one's spouse and children but by a strong sense of subjective happiness in marriage. The

---

[13] John Paul II, *Familiaris consortio*, no 13.

turning away from a Judeo-Christian view and the loss of the Catholic understanding of sacramental marriage were facilitated by the significant movement away from faith, the Church's teaching on sexual morality, and regular church attendance, which are proven to be protective of marital commitment, happiness, and fulfillment.

The unfortunate reality in marital therapy today is that many professionals do not embrace the traditional Judeo-Christian view of marriage and are overly influenced instead by the selfishness in the culture. They often fail to help spouses grow in self-knowledge to identify the emotional wounds and personality weaknesses from each spouse's family of origin or previous relationships. Marital therapists who have not worked on their own family-of-origin wounds and weaknesses and who have not mastered, for example, selfishness and anger in their own lives will have difficulty assisting clients in uncovering and resolving these problems. In addition, therapists may not understand the benefits of forgiveness, and subsequently, may fail to incorporate forgiveness therapy when working with spouses.

A major study of six hundred couples highlighted the pitfalls of marital therapy: those who received marital counseling were two to three times more likely to divorce than couples who did not have counseling. James D. Wright, a sociologist at the University of Central Florida and one of the authors of this research, said that the counseling profession too frequently tries to help clients through divorce rather than helping them repair their marriages. Until there is evidence that marital counseling helps couples strengthen their marriages, he said, couples should be wary of marital counseling, and states should not make it mandatory.[14]

[14] Steven L. Nock, Laura Ann Sanchez, and James D. Wright, *Covenant Marriage: The Movement to Reclaim Tradition in America* (New Brunswick, N.J.: Rutgers University Press, 2008), 122.

Therefore, caution should be taken with respect to the decision to seek professional marital counseling. I recommend it when prior discussions with couples in good marriages or with clergy have not been helpful in reducing marital stress and with the strong suggestion that the couple seek a counselor who is sympathetic to their faith and their desire to persevere in their marriage.

Contraception

Since its introduction in 1962, the pill has promoted a general "contraceptive mentality" that has undermined marriage. While the divorce rate had been going up slowly in the 1900s, it doubled between 1965 and 1975. A 1977 study conducted by Robert Michael at the Center for Economic Analysis of Human Behavior and Social Institutions examined this sudden jump and concluded that a large portion of this increase could be directly attributed to the increased use of contraceptives.

Contraceptives have made marriages less child centered and have led to a weakening of marital commitment. These two things go hand in hand, as Father Cormac Burke, a civil and canon lawyer, has explained:

> Conjugal love, then, needs the support represented by children. Children strengthen the goodness of the bond of marriage, so that it does not give way under the strains that follow on the inevitable wane and disappearance of effortless romantic love. The bond of marriage—which God wants no man to break—is then constituted not simply by the variables of personal love and sentiment between husband and wife, but more and more by their children, each child being one more added strand giving strength to the bond.[15]

[15] Cormac Burke, *Covenanted Happiness: Love and Commitment in Marriage* (Strongsville, Ohio: Scepter, 1999), 106.

The divorce of a very close friend can increase a person's risk of getting divorced by 75 percent. By the time a couple has a third child, however, the effect of another's divorce becomes insignificant, and by the fifth child, it completely vanishes.[16] These findings suggest that children do indeed have a protective effect on marriage.

The psychological and emotional states that go along with using contraception can weaken the marital bond. These include a diminished trust in God and one's spouse and an increase in selfishness. Also, when the physical side effects of contraception are endured by only one spouse in order to be sexually available to the other spouse, anger and resentment can result.

The proponents of fertility awareness methods of family planning, most often called Natural Family Planning (NFP), have long claimed that practitioners of these methods have lower divorce rates than those who use contraception. A 2015 study tested this claim and found that "among women who ever used NFP, only 9.6 percent were currently divorced compared with the 14.4 percent who were currently divorced among the women who never used NFP." The study also found that having an abortion, being sterilized, or using contraception "increased the likelihood of divorce—up to two times", while frequent church attendance was associated with less divorce.[17]

Sadly, the influence of the contraceptive mentality on Catholic couples, family members, mental health

[16] Rose McDermott, James Fowler, and Nicholas Christakis, "Breaking Up is Hard to Do, Unless Everyone Else Is Doing It Too: Social Network Effects on Divorce in a Longitudinal Sample", *Social Forces* 92, no. 2 (December 2013): 511.

[17] Richard J. Fehring, "The Influence of Contraception, Abortion, and Natural Family Planning on Divorce Rates as Found in the 2006–2010 National Survey of Family Growth", *Linacre Quarterly* 82, no. 3 (August 2015): 273–82, https://www.ncbi.nlm.nih.gov/pmc/articles/PMC4536625/.

professionals, clergy, and religious has weakened their ability to defend marriage and to encourage couples under stress
to work on relying upon and remaining loyal to their sacramental bond while attempting to resolve their conflicts.

Recommendations for Severe Marital Stress

Despite recent reports that the divorce rate is stabilizing, a
2014 report in the journal *Demography* provides evidence
that the divorce rate has doubled over the past two decades
among people over thirty-five.[18] Given the severity of the
divorce trend, Catholics must work harder to help couples
through times of marital distress. In doing so, we can be
encouraged by the hopeful words of Saint John Paul II:

> Whenever a couple is going through difficulties, the
> sympathy of Pastors, and of the other faithful must be
> combined with clarity and fortitude in remembering that
> conjugal love is the way to work out a positive solution
> to their crisis. Given that God has united them by means
> of an indissoluble bond, the husband and wife by utiliz-
> ing all their human resources, together with good will,
> and by, above all, confiding in the assistance of divine
> grace, can and should emerge from their moments of
> crisis renewed and strengthened.[19]

It is vitally important that couples under severe marital
stress use caution and prudence in deciding in whom they
will confide to share their pain and to seek advice. They

---

[18] S. Kennedy and S. Ruggles, "Breaking Up Is Hard to Count: The Rise of
Divorce in the United States, 1980–2010", *Demography* 51, no. 2 (April 2014):
587–98, http://doi.org/10.1007/s13524-013-0270-9.

[19] John Paul II, Address to the Prelate Auditors, Officials and Advocates of
the Tribunal of the Roman Rota (January 28, 2002), no. 5.

should consider communicating only with those who have good marriages, who support the Church's teaching on marriage, and who have not embraced the pervasive divorce mentality. We recommend that couples under stress first seek the support of a friend or another couple who have a healthy marriage.

For spouses experiencing marital problems, I recommend the Marriage Disciples apostolate of the Alexander House, which brings hope to troubled marriages at the parish level. The apostolate is now present in more than one hundred parishes, and one hopes that this vital apostolate will continue to expand throughout the Church. I also recommend participation in the outstanding Retrouvaille program. In addition, consultation with a parish priest can be beneficial.

Finally, if all these steps do not result in an improvement in the marriage, consultation with a mental health professional could be considered. I recommend that spouses seek a therapist who is loyal to the Church's teaching on marriage, believes that marital conflicts can be resolved, and has had success in helping spouses to stay together.

The Virtue of Justice

The good news is that most divorces can be avoided and marital love can be rediscovered. The process of healing, however, is demanding. Often it is also humbling, as spouses face deeply buried emotional pain and character weaknesses that they had previously ignored. As they embark on this difficult process, the first virtue that I ask couples to consider is justice. People are often surprised at this, as if justice and love were contrary to each other. But as Pope Benedict explained, "If we love others with charity, then first of all we are just towards them. Not only is justice not extraneous to charity, not only is it not an alternative or parallel path to charity: justice is inseparable from charity, and intrinsic to it."[20]

The *Catechism* defines justice as "the moral virtue that consists in the constant and firm will to give their due to God and neighbor", who in the case of marriage is one's spouse and children (1807). The just person respects the rights of others, seeks harmony in human relationships, and protects the common good. Often mentioned in Scripture, he is "distinguished by habitual right thinking and the uprightness of his conduct toward his neighbor".

The virtue of justice imposes on spouses the obligation to work hard to heal their marriage, to be loyal to their children's need for a stable union, and to persevere in the vows they made to each other and to God. I ask couples thinking of divorce to take two years to do everything they can to save their marriage. Those who do so often rediscover the goodness in each other. They subsequently have a deeper love for each other and a greater appreciation for the Sacrament of Matrimony.

Given the severe harm to children from divorce, young children and teenagers should be allowed the freedom to tell a parent, "If you loved me [or us], you would work to save the marriage and the family" or, "You are not doing enough to help the marriage, and you need to do more." Many adult children of divorce have expressed deep regret that they did not exhort their parents to work harder to save their marriages.

Parents, siblings, in-laws, and friends should consider their responsibility in justice to make similar requests to a spouse who is considering divorce. Often, the views of the

[20] Benedict XVI, Encyclical Letter *Caritas in veritate* (June 29, 2009), no. 6.

spouse who is committed and loyal to the marriage and the welfare of the children are ignored by family members, friends, and marriage counselors, and loyal spouses are told that they have no choice but to accept the divorce.

Clergy should also encourage spouses to work harder on improving themselves and their marriage. Spouses who want a divorce will often tell a priest or a mental health professional that they have already worked hard for many years on trying to improve their marriages. While this might be true in a small number of marriages, rarely do such spouses have adequate self-knowledge about their weaknesses. Sometimes spouses who push for a divorce feel like innocent victims who have reached the limit of their endurance. These spouses need to be assured that low-level conflicts can be resolved, particularly when faith and forgiveness are incorporated in the steps toward reconciliation.

Faith

Faith helps to save many marriages on the brink of divorce. Research at the University of Virginia led by the late Dr. Steven Nock has shown that religious faith reduces the likelihood of divorce in three ways. First, faith helps spouses to perceive God as the benefactor and the protector of marriage. Second, faith gives spouses a sense of duty to God to develop strong relationships and communication skills within the family. Third, confidence that marriage is a sacred union between the two spouses and God helps spouses to manage severe marital stress, often with great success.[21]

[21] Nock, Sanchez, and Wright, *Covenant Marriage*, p. 126.

In my experience, when spouses recognize the divine purpose in their marriage and the assistance that they can receive from God if they turn to him, they are more hopeful about overcoming thoughts of divorce and engaging in the hard work of uncovering and addressing the wounds and the character weaknesses that have caused conflict. Faith is a great gift in marriage that many Catholic couples have not fully unpacked. It provides access to another, and better, source of comfort, strength, and love than reliance on themselves.

Research has shown that prayer can help in the healing of disease;[22] similarly, in my forty years of clinical experience with Catholic couples, I have found prayer for oneself and one's spouse to be beneficial in helping to diminish and often resolving the serious conflicts that lead spouses to consider divorce. Prayer often fosters greater compassion for the suffering of one's spouse due to past emotional hurts and personality weaknesses.

One couple who had been on the brink of separation and divorce many times over the course of their thirty-year marriage explained how faith and prayer had helped their marriage to survive. Each spouse was a strongly passionate individual. The husband had grown up with a selfish father, and the wife with a controlling mother. The spouses then repeated these weaknesses in their marriage, which produced serious ongoing conflicts. In one session the husband said to me, "Doc, I'm sure that you're wondering how our marriage has lasted thirty years", which was exactly what I had been thinking. He did not wait for my response, but took out his rosary beads and said,

[22] Patrick Fagan, "Why Religion Matters: The Impact of Religious Practice on Social Stability", *Civil Society*, January 25,1996, Heritage Foundation, https://www.heritage.org/civil-society/report/why-religion-matters-the -impact-religious-practice-social-stability.

"We have survived as a couple because we love each other and, more importantly, because we pray a Rosary together every night for our marriage and our children. Our Lady has sustained our marriage."

This couple's perseverance in love, with the help of faith, hope, and prayer, has made their marriage a witness to the love of God, not only for them but for all mankind. As Saint John Paul II wrote, "To bear witness to the inestimable value of the indissolubility and fidelity of marriage is one of the most precious and most urgent tasks of Christian couples in our time."[23]

[23] John Paul II, *Familiaris consortio*, no. 20.

11

Loyalty Lessens the Retreat from Marriage

[Sexuality] is realized in a truly human way only if it is an integral part of the love by which a man and woman commit themselves totally to one another until death.... The only "place" in which this self-giving in its whole truth is made possible is marriage.

—Saint John Paul II

The wisdom from above is first pure, then peaceable, gentle, open to reason, full of mercy and good fruits, without uncertainty or insincerity.

—James 3:17

The major goal of this chapter is to help Catholic parents, siblings, relatives, friends, educators, and clergy to grow in the virtue of loyalty toward those who are cohabiting, those who plan to cohabit, and those who, cohabiting or not, lack a desire to marry. The call to loyalty is also addressed to couples who are living together outside of marriage or considering it.

This application of the virtue of loyalty requires accurate knowledge about cohabitation and marriage, and the

John Paul II, Apostolic Exhortation on the Role of the Christian Family in the Modern World *Familiaris consortio* (November 22, 1981), no. 11.

communication of this information to those in need of it. Such loyalty is motivated by the love that wishes the best for others. The psychological risks to those living in cohabiting unions and to children born into and living in these unions, are uncovered and addressed, as are the major causes of cohabitation. The habit of loyalty in speaking the truth in love is described.

The "Cohabitation Revolution"

Cohabitation has been steadily increasing in the United States. The National Center for Health Statistics' 2018 report on cohabitation, based on data collected from 2011 to 2015, revealed that 67 percent of those currently married had cohabited before marriage with one or more partners. It also found that, as of 2015,

- 44.9 percent of women and 43.5 percent of men were married.
- 38.0 percent of women and 40.6 percent of men were unmarried and not cohabiting.
- 44 percent of the currently cohabiting group and 20 percent of the neither cohabiting nor married group had already lived with two or more partners.
- The percent of women ages nineteen to forty-four who have cohabited has increased by 82 percent over the past twenty-three years.
- The increase in illegitimate births in the United States since 1980 has mostly taken pace in cohabiting unions.[1]

[1] C. N. Nugent and J. Daugherty, "A Demographic, Attitudinal, and Behavioral Profile of Cohabiting Adults in the United States, 2011–2015", *National Health Statistics Reports* 111 (May 2018): 1–6.

Cohabitation has become a central part of the family landscape for both children and adults, so much so that family and marriage scholars have characterized this development as a "cohabitation revolution".[2]

The Causes of the Cohabitation Revolution

Pope John Paul II observed the growing practice of cohabitation throughout the world, and he noted that from place to place the reasons for it varied:

> Some people consider themselves almost forced into a free union by difficult economic, cultural or religious situations, on the grounds that, if they contracted a regular marriage, they would be exposed to some form of harm, would lose economic advantages, would be discriminated against, etc. In other cases, however, one encounters people who scorn, rebel against or reject society, the institution of the family and the social and political order, or who are solely seeking pleasure. Then there are those who are driven to such situations by extreme ignorance or poverty, sometimes by a conditioning due to situations of real injustice, or by a certain psychological immaturity that makes them uncertain or afraid to enter into a stable and definitive union. In some countries, traditional customs presume that the true and proper marriage will take place only after a period of cohabitation and the birth of the first child.[3]

[2] Pamela J. Smock and Wendy D. Manning, "New Couples, New Families: The Cohabitation Revolution in the United States", in *Families as They Really Are*, ed. Barbara Risman (New York: W. W. Norton, 2010), 131–39.

[3] John Paul II, *Familiaris consortio*, no. 81.

One factor in the growth of cohabitation in the United States is that the world of entertainment and the lives of celebrities have normalized and even glorified it, while people have rejected traditional wisdom about the benefits of marriage for spouses, children, and society. Sociologist Dr. Bradford Wilcox, director of the National Marriage Project at the University of Virginia, wrote, "One of the primary reasons for getting married—starting a family—is increasingly viewed as a relic of the past."[4] Sadly, this is also true among many Catholics, and surely a contributing factor is the number of clergy, religious, educators, and other adults who for decades have undermined the Church's liberating truth about sexual morality.

In my clinical experience over the past forty years, I have found the following causes of cohabitation:

- Profound selfishness with distaste for sacrificial giving
- Absence of loyalty in loving relationships
- Desire to dominate
- Acceptance of contraception and of the use of another person as a sexual object
- Pornography use
- Ignorance about the Sacrament of Marriage
- Financial fears of not being able to provide for a family
- A distorted notion of freedom and responsibility
- Fear of divorce and, consequently, commitment
- Lack of faith and trust in the Lord with the challenges of life

These fears contribute to the present retreat from marriage and to the decision to cohabit, which does not require a

---

[4] W. Bradford Wilcox, *Why Marriage Matters: Thirty Conclusions from the Social Sciences* (West Chester, Pa.: Broadway Publications, 2011), 7–9.

complete commitment. In a study by Wilcox, 41 percent of cohabiting men reported that "they are not 'completely committed' to their live-in girlfriends."[5]

Cohabitation Myths

The rapid increase of cohabitation has led to widespread cultural acceptance of the practice. As a result, many people believe that cohabitation is psychologically healthy, prepares young adults for marriage, and helps couples to weed out negative relationships before making a lifelong marital commitment.

The harsh reality is that these low-commitment, high-autonomy relationships are not a psychologically healthy way to prepare for marriage. David Popenoe, former director of the National Marriage Project at Rutgers University, and Barbara Dafoe Whitehead, author of *The Divorce Culture*, have described the risks of cohabitation:

- Living together before marriage increases the risk of breaking up after marriage.
- Living together outside of marriage increases the risk of domestic violence for women and the risk of physical and sexual abuse for children.
- Unmarried couples have lower levels of happiness and well-being than married couples.[6]

---

[5] W. Bradford Wilcox, "Men and Women Often Expect Different Things When They Move in Together", *Atlantic*, July 8, 2013, http://www.theatlantic .com/sexes/archive/2013/07/men-and-women-ofen-expect-different-things -when-they-move-in-together/277571/.

[6] David Popenoe and Barbara Dafoe Whitehead, *Should We Live Together? What Young Adults Need to Know about Cohabitation before Marriage*, 2nd ed. (Piscataway, N.J.: National Marriage Project, 2002), http://nationalmarriageproject .org/wp-content/uploads/2013/01/ShouldWeLiveTogether.pdf.

Cohabitation arrangements tend to be short-lived, resulting in deep emotional scars to the couple and to any children who might have resulted from the relationship. A 2013 study on 12,279 women, ages fifteen to forty-four, found that the median duration of first cohabitation was twenty-two months, yet nearly 20 percent of women became pregnant and gave birth in the first year of a first premarital cohabitation.[7]

After leaving a cohabitation relationship, young adults frequently express strong anger with their parents, siblings, friends, teachers, and clergy who supported their moving in with a boyfriend or girlfriend without warning them of the risks. Sadly, many of those involved believed the myth that cohabitation was harmless if not beneficial. Yet the harm done by cohabitation has been widely documented; thus, it is high time for this information to be shared with young people, and if possible, before they make this serious mistake.

The Harm of Cohabiting Unions

In my clinical experience, the depression of men and women who are or were cohabiting most often relates to the realization that their significant other has or had no desire for a permanent, lifelong commitment and children. To say the least, they are dissatisfied with their relationship.

Studies have shown that cohabiting couples experience less relationship satisfaction than married individuals do.[8]

[7] C.E. Copen, K. Daniels, and W.D. Mosher, "First Premarital Cohabitation in the United States: 2006–2010 National Survey of Family Growth", *National Health Statistics Reports* 64 (April 2013): 1–14.

[8] Susan L. Brown, "The Effect of Union Type on Psychological Well-Being: Depression among Cohabitors versus Marrieds", *Journal of Health and Social Behavior* 41, no. 3 (2000): 247.

As either a cause or an effect of relationship dissatisfaction, after controlling for other factors, cohabiters are more than twice as likely to engage in infidelity as married people are.[9] And there is an even darker side to cohabitation: women in cohabiting relationships are more likely to suffer physical and sexual abuse than married women, and they are nine times more likely to be killed by their partner than married women are.[10]

Cohabiting couples have a diminished likelihood of being happily married later. The overwhelming majority of studies show that cohabitation before marriage is associated with poorer odds of stability and happiness in marriage.[11] Cohabitation before marriage is associated with lower marital satisfaction, dedication, and confidence as well as increased negative communication and a higher divorce rate.[12] In fact, one study found a 50 percent increased risk of divorce associated with premarital cohabitation.[13]

As Saint John Paul II concluded about the negative effects of cohabitation:

Each of these elements presents the Church with arduous pastoral problems, by reason of the serious consequences

[9] W. D. Mosher, A. Chandra, and J. Jones, "Sexual Behavior and Selected Health Measures: Men and Women 15–44 Years of Age, United States, 2002", *Advance Data* (September 15, 2005): 1–55.

[10] T. K. Shackelford, "Cohabitation, Marriage, and Murder: Women Killing by Male Romantic Partners", *Aggressive Behavior* 27, no. 4 (2001): 284–91.

[11] Scott M. Stanley, Galena Kline Rhoades, and Howard J. Markman, "Sliding versus Deciding: Inertia and the Premarital Cohabitation Effect", *Family Relations* 55, no. 4 (October 2006): 499–509.

[12] Galena Kline Rhoades, Scott M. Stanley, and Howard J. Markman, "The Pre-Engagement Cohabitation Effect: A Replication and Extension of Previous Findings", *Journal of Family Psychology* 23, no 1 (February 2009): 107–11.

[13] Claire M. Kamp Dush, Catherine L. Cohan, and Paul R. Amato, "The Relationship between Cohabitation and Marital Quality and Stability: Change across Cohorts?", *Journal of Marriage and Family* 65, no. 3 (August 2003): 539–49.

deriving from them, both religious and moral (the loss of the religious sense of marriage seen in the light of the Covenant of God with His people; deprivation of the grace of the sacrament; grave scandal), and also social consequences (the destruction of the concept of the family; the weakening of the sense of fidelity, also towards society; possible psychological damage to the children; the strengthening of selfishness).[14]

Cohabitation and Posttraumatic Stress Disorder

No small number of Catholic female singles report anxiety, panic episodes, sadness, and anger after the ending of a cohabiting relationship of one or two years' duration. Not infrequently, these young women had hoped that when they moved in with their boyfriends, the arrangement would lead to marriage and children. Instead, the women eventually and painfully realized that the men they shared their lives with would not marry them. Then the women's trust in and romantic feelings for the men decreased, as did their desire for sexual intimacy with them. The fact that we see more women with these feelings of betrayal than men could be an indication of an insight of Saint John Paul II: "A 'marital' sexual relationship outside the framework of marriage is always objectively a wrong done to the woman."[15] In some cases, the roles are reversed, and the cohabiting woman does not want to marry her live-in boyfriend, who wants to marry her.

[14] John Paul II, *Familiaris consortio*, no. 81.
[15] Karol Wojtyla, *Love and Responsibility* (San Francisco: Ignatius Press, 1993), 221.

The dissolution of a cohabiting relationship has been referred to as a "divorce equivalent", because the couple often experiences the same posttraumatic stress disorder as do married people who divorce. The emotional pain in these young women and young men, however, can go even deeper than that experienced with a divorce. They often feel that they were used sexually and in others ways, and then rejected. They have experienced an injustice on an existential level, underlying the truth of another insight of John Paul II: "For to be just always means giving others what is rightly due them. A person's rightful due is to be treated as an object of love, not as an object for use."[16] The resulting sadness, anxiety, insecurity, and anger often lead previously cohabiting people to seek the help of mental health professionals, who sometimes prescribe antidepressant and antianxiety medications.

Depression, Suicide, and Anger Risks from Hormonal Contraceptive Use

It is safe to assume that many cohabiting couples use some form of birth control. Given that the pill is the most common form in the United States, it also safe to suppose that a great number of cohabiting women use it. When they present depression symptoms after a breakup with a live-in boyfriend, contraceptives should not be ruled out as having a contributing role.

Two studies demonstrate risks of depression and suicide particularly in younger women who use the pill and other hormonal contraceptives. A 2016 study of more than one million women living in Denmark found a higher risk of

[16] Ibid., 42.

depression among users of hormonal contraception compared with nonusers.[17] A study by the same researchers the following year compared nearly half a million women who used hormonal contraceptives with women who never used them, and these results showed that users were at greater risk for suicide.[18]

Harm to Children

The share of births to unmarried mothers doubled between 1980 and 2013, with 43 percent of births between 2009 and 2013 occurring to single or cohabiting mothers. During this period there was a more than 300 percent increase in the share of births to cohabiting mothers, whereas the share of births to single mothers remained largely unchanged. The majority of unmarried births occurred to cohabiting rather than single mothers.[19]

One might think that more children being born to cohabiting mothers than simply single mothers is some kind of improvement. But after reviewing a large body of research examining the children of cohabiting couples, the American College of Pediatricians has outlined

[17] Charlotte Wessel Skovlund, Lina Steinrud Mørch, Lars Vedel Kessing, and Øjvind Lidegaard, "Association of Hormonal Contraception with Depression", *JAMA Psychiatry* 73, no. 11 (November 2016): 1154–62, http://doi.org/10.1001/jamapsychiatry.2016.2387.

[18] Charlotte Wessel Skovlund, Lina Steinrud Mørch, Lars Vedel Kessing, and Øjvind Lidegaard, "Association of Hormonal Contraception with Suicide Attempts and Suicide", *American Journal of Psychiatry* 175, no. 4 (April 2018): 336–42, https://doi.org/10.1176/appi.ajp.2017.17060616.

[19] Wendy D. Manning, Susan L. Brown, and Bark Stykes, *Trends in Births to Single and Cohabiting Mothers, 1980–2013* (Bowling Green, Ohio: National Center for Family and Marriage Research, 2015), https://www.bgsu.edu/content/dam/BGSU/college-of-arts-and-sciences/NCFMR/documents/FP/FP-15-03-birth-trends-single-cohabiting-moms.pdf.

a number of negative effects of cohabitation on children. According to their report, children born prior to, during, or after parental cohabitation are at increased risk for premature birth; school failure; lower education; more poverty during childhood and lower incomes as adults; more incarceration and behavior problems; single parenthood; medical neglect and chronic health problems, both medical and psychiatric; more substance, alcohol, and tobacco abuse; and more child abuse. The report concluded that cohabitation is inherently unstable and carries a high cost to children's physical and psychological development.[20]

The Benefits of Marriage

A person is rarely motivated to avoid something simply because of negative effects suffered by someone else. People are, however, drawn to something they believe will be good for them. Thus, to deter young adults from cohabitation, those close to them should not only discuss the harm it does but should also demonstrate the good of marriage.

Tyler J. VanderWeele, director of the Human Flourishing Program at Harvard University, has written on the benefits of marriage that have been demonstrated by countless studies:

Marriage is associated with higher life satisfaction and greater affective happiness. Evidence moreover suggests that marriage is associated with better mental health, physical health, and longevity, even controlling for baseline health. Concerning character and virtue, although understudied

[20] Patricia Lee June, "Cohabitation: Effects of Cohabitation and Other Non-Marital Sexual Activity on Children, Part 2", American College of Pediatricians, July 2014, https://www.acpeds.org/the-college-speaks/position-statements/societal-issues/cohabitation-part-2-of-2.

and current outcome measures are inadequate, there is longitudinal evidence that marriage is associated with higher level of personal growth, and with a reduction in crime for those at high risk. It is also associated with higher levels of meaning and purpose in life. Marriage is moreover associated longitudinally with higher levels of positive relationships with others, higher levels of perceived social support, and lower levels of loneliness. Marriage likewise tends to be associated with better financial outcomes, even controlling for baseline financial status and education.[21]

These are the medical, psychological, and financial benefits of marriage, but the Church teaches that there is a yet deeper good of marriage, from which these other benefits flow.

When entered into fully, marriage provides the unconditional, lifelong love that every person needs and desires. It " 'reveals' and 'fulfills' the wise and loving plan of God for the married couple, giving them a mysterious and real share in the very love with which God Himself loves humanity."[22] Within the Sacrament of Matrimony, true Christian personality growth is realized, especially when both husband and wife commit themselves to addressing their personality weaknesses and growing in virtues through their mutual help and through God's abundant grace. A greater awareness of this vision for marriage can diminish the cohabitation trend.

Loyalty, Love, and Truth

Loyalty is unswerving love for those we care about. It is an act of both loyalty and love to help others to do what

[21] Tyler J. VanderWeele, "On the Promotion of Human Flourishing", *Proceedings of the National Academy of Sciences* 114, no. 31 (August 2017): 8148–56, https://www.ncbi.nlm.nih.gov/pmc/articles/PMC5547610/.

[22] John Paul II, *Familiaris consortio*, no. 51.

is right by setting a good example and offering wise counsel based on the truth. "Each person finds his good by adherence to God's plan for him.... To defend the truth, to articulate it with humility and conviction, and to bear witness to it in life are therefore exacting and indispensable forms of charity."[23]

Our children, relatives, and friends who are young adults need help with discerning the way God is calling them to serve him. For most of them, that vocation is marriage; but hearing this calling and accepting it is difficult when so many other voices are saying that marriage is neither necessary nor desirable. "It is thus becoming a social and even economic necessity once more to hold up to future generations the beauty of marriage and the family, and the fact that these institutions correspond to the deepest needs and dignity of the person."[24]

Loyalty in Parents

As the first educators of their children, parents have a mission from God to witness to the truth about sexuality, marriage, and family life to their children. Along with this mission, God gives abundant grace.

> For Christian parents the mission to educate, a mission rooted, as we have said, in their participation in God's creating activity, has a new specific source in the sacrament of marriage, which consecrates them for the strictly Christian education of their children: that is to say, it calls upon them to share in the very authority and love of God the Father and Christ the Shepherd, and in the motherly love of the Church, and it enriches them with wisdom,

---

[23] Benedict XVI, Encyclical Letter *Caritas in veritate* (June 29, 2009), no. 1.
[24] Ibid., no. 44.

counsel, fortitude and all the other gifts of the Holy Spirit in order to help the children in their growth as human beings and as Christians.[25]

Parents should therefore be bold in sharing with even their adult children the harm of cohabitation and the benefits of the Sacrament of Matrimony.

The major obstacles to such boldness are fears of being criticized for daring to challenge the widespread acceptance of sex outside of marriage and of losing the love and closeness of their children. But due to the ignorance or rejection of Catholic morality in many Catholic schools and parishes since the late 1960s, parents need to recognize that if they do not uphold God's loving plan for the family, their children may never hear about it anywhere else. They need to fortify themselves for this act of loyalty by realizing that more than their children's feelings are at stake.

Even the American College of Pediatricians urges parents to have tough conversations with their teens about the risks of sex outside of marriage and of cohabitation. On its website is the following statement: "Sound research suggests that couples contemplating cohabitation should exercise extreme caution given the negative effects such an arrangement has upon the individual, the relationship and any conceived children."[26] When the surrounding culture both inside and outside the Catholic Church frowned upon extramarital sex and encouraged marriage, Catholics did not need "sound research" to tell them that cohabitation was a bad idea. But given current social trends, Catholics need all the help they can get to

[25] John Paul II, *Familiaris consortio*, no. 38.

[26] American College of Pediatricians, "Effect of Cohabitation on the Individuals and Couple", https://www.acpeds.org/wordpress/wp-content/uploads/Effects-of-Cohabitation-on-the-Individuals-and-Couple.pdf.

have enough confidence in Church teaching to pass it on to their children.

A helpful resource for parents in this task is the Vatican document *The Truth and Meaning of Human Sexuality*, which illuminates the necessity of reinvigorating our love for that "old-fashioned" virtue called chastity:

> The love for chastity, which parents help to form, favors mutual respect between man and woman and provides a capacity for compassion, tolerance, generosity, and above all, a spirit of sacrifice, without which love cannot endure. Children will thus come to marriage with that realistic wisdom about which Saint Paul speaks when he teaches that husband and wife must continually give way to one another in love, cherishing one another with mutual patience and affection.[27]

Chastity is not prudishness. Rather, it is the virtue that moderates our desire for sexual pleasure so that we do not use and abuse other people for our own gratification. In this time when we are discovering rampant sexual abuse in every institution of our society, including the Church, the moment has come to relearn how to cultivate this necessary virtue.

Not only do parents need to grow in this virtue themselves and to encourage it in their children, but they also need to help their children discern whether the persons they love and perhaps even desire to live with are capable of embracing this virtue. If parents believe that their child's significant other is overly selfish, they should recommend that the child consider addressing this issue before going further in the relationship. If the boyfriend or girlfriend

[27] Pontifical Council of the Family, *The Truth and Meaning of Human Sexuality* (December 8, 1995), no. 31.

shows a lack of willingness to work on this common personality weakness, parents should recommend that their
child end the relationship. They should have no reserva-
tion about speaking openly about their concern that their
child is being used. If their child is the one pushing for a
sexual relationship or a cohabiting arrangement, the parents should confront their son or daughter for selfishly
using another person.

The loyalty of parents to their child should extend to
offering their honest opinion about the conduct of their
child or their child's significant other. They should be
frank if they think that a child's boyfriend or girlfriend
seems incapable of making a commitment to marriage,
parenthood, and the sacrificial self-giving required of
both. If the person has had family-of-origin traumas,
parents should coach their child to bring up these issues
so that the person can find healing, and they should explain that it is very difficult to do so without a spiritual
outlook on life.

If a child is already cohabiting and manifesting symptoms of anxiety or depression, loyalty to that child's emotional, psychological, and spiritual health would lead a
parent to recommend ending that relationship, forgiving the significant other, seeking the peace that comes
from Confession, and starting afresh. In some cases, professional counseling might also be recommended. Too
often, well-meaning parents betray their children by
remaining silent.

Loyalty in Singles

Catholic singles who are considering a cohabiting arrangement, or are already cohabiting, owe it to themselves to
consider the wisdom of the Catholic Church regarding

marriage with an open mind and thus grow in their capacity to give and to receive the true love that their hearts desire. The writings of Saint John Paul II that have been cited throughout this book are a good place to start, and so are the many materials that explain his Theology of the Body. This theology is based on what it means to be human and on the needs of the human heart.

The desire to live with someone one loves can be a positive indication that this person could potentially become one's partner in life—one's beloved wife or husband and the mother or the father of one's children. An intense romantic, sexual relationship with the use of contraception, however, can impair the ability to evaluate objectively the personality and the compatibility of another person. Sexual activity can supplant the needed conversations about beliefs, values, and goals that are so necessary for making a decision about one's future spouse.

It is far safer psychologically and spiritually to develop a special, even romantic, friendship first, one in which a shared vision for a common future can be explored and sacrificial self-giving love can develop, before any big steps in the relationship are taken prematurely. Often singles push for cohabitation for their own, sometimes unconscious, selfish reasons, such as the desire to have sex without commitment, the need to dominate, the fear of being alone, and the fear of the commitment and the responsibilities that go along with family life.

In many cases, one or more of the following may be reasons for these weaknesses:

- Extreme self-centeredness
- Divorce of one's parents
- Lack of happily married role models
- Lack of confidence in one's ability to provide for a family

- Fear of pregnancy
- Mistrust of the opposite sex

Singles considering cohabitation should look carefully at themselves to see if they have any of these weaknesses. To be loyal to each other is to want the best for each other, including continued personal growth. If one or both parties do not have the maturity to grow in self-knowledge, what does that say about their prospects for happiness together? If they do have what it takes, they should be encouraged to consider marriage, for only in committed unconditional love can a man and a woman truly grow together into the people God created them to be.

Loyalty in Clergy, Religious, and Educators

The painful truth needs to be faced that vast numbers of Catholic clergy, religious, and educators have been disloyal to young people by their silence about or their dissent from the Church's teaching on marriage and sexual morality. In many cases, no doubt, those with the responsibility to teach and to form young people were ignorant of the beauty of that teaching and saw it only as an unnatural, impossible, shame-inducing standard. Saint Josemaría Escrivá described another reason for the failure to uphold the truth: "There is a great love of comfort, and at times a great irresponsibility, hidden behind the attitude of those in authority who flee from the sorrow of correcting, making the excuse that they want to avoid the suffering of others."[28]

Now that fallout of the sexual revolution is as clear as day, it is time for Catholic leaders and educators to reevaluate the splendor of the Church's teaching and offer it intact to the young people so in need of it.

---

[28] Josemaría Escrivá, *The Forge* (Strongsville, Ohio: Scepter, 2011), no. 577.

Healing of Wounds

No matter how much people have hurt themselves by making bad decisions regarding sexual relationships, the good news is that their wounds can be healed through the mercy and love of God. The healing process after the breakup of a cohabiting couple is similar to the healing process after a divorce, which requires understanding the serious weaknesses that undermined the relationship and forgiving them.

Forgiveness is challenging, especially for women who often feel that the "best years" of their lives, meaning those for starting a family, had been stolen by the illusion that their live-in boyfriends would eventually marry them. In some cases, their boyfriends were indulging in pornography, substance abuse, and other selfish behaviors while the women were keeping house for them. But the inability of young men to mature into the kind of men who can become responsible husbands and fathers is often linked to family-of-origin problems and traumas. The work of forgiveness often requires uncovering those weaknesses and the anger that built up over them. In addition to anger, there is often deep sadness and fear of betrayal.

In such cases, one must realize that forgiving and moving on is impossible without giving one's powerlessness over sadness and anger to the Lord. Forgiveness then becomes a process, in which there is a gradual decrease in these strong emotions.

The heartbreak experienced after cohabitation can often lead to a desire for Catholic marriage and family life. Parents and friends of previously cohabiting couples can do much to build their confidence that with the Lord that desire can be fulfilled.

12

Humility Fosters Self-Knowledge

Humility is a necessary condition for man's interior "harmony": for man's "interior" beauty.

—Saint John Paul II

With the humble is wisdom.

—Proverbs 11:2

The goal of this chapter is to impart greater awareness of the lifelong influence exerted by the people who most affect one's personality prior to and during marriage—one's parents. It goes without saying that the good habits acquired from unconsciously modeling after parents are a positive. The unconscious modeling after a parental weakness, however, can significantly interfere with maintaining a healthy personality and healthy relationships with one's spouse and children. Research has shown that approximately 70 percent of adult psychological conflicts originate in childhood and adolescence.

From a Christian perspective, the role model for a healthy personality is the Lord. Growth in becoming more like Jesus requires humility, which involves the knowledge of both strengths and weaknesses. This self-knowledge leads to gratitude for the gifts we have received from God

John Paul II, General Audience (November 22, 1978), no. 5.

through our parents. It also motivates us to uncover our psychological and spiritual weaknesses and to cooperate with God's grace in conquering them through growth in virtue, which is a lifelong task.

The bad habits modeled after parents that most commonly cause conflict and unhappiness in marriage are the tendencies to be selfish, to control, to lose one's temper, to worry, to be emotionally distant, and to mistrust others. The process described in this chapter can help spouses to break free from the past and to make progress toward the wholeness they desire—for themselves and for their marriage.

Cesar and Francesca

Both Cesar and Francesca had deep faith, yet they both became extremely frustrated about the difficulties in their marriage. Cesar had even wondered if marital separation might be needed because he strongly believed that his wife was solely responsible for their problems. His major complaint was that she had become increasingly selfish and less loving and responsible toward the family. He was particularly concerned that her self-absorption was causing her to be too permissive with their two children.

Francesca, on the other hand, felt that Cesar had been treating her in a disrespectful and controlling manner throughout their twenty years of marriage. She disagreed completely with Cesar's analysis of their problems and thought that she had been a loyal and responsible wife and mother.

Self-Knowledge

Both Francesca and Cesar were making the common mistake of blaming the other spouse for the problems in their marriage. They both needed to grow in self-knowledge, the starting point in the discovery of the truth that Jesus said "will make you free" (Jn 8:32). Knowing the truth about oneself was widely valued in the ancient world as the path to wisdom, as Pope John Paul II reminded us: "The admonition *Know yourself* was carved on the temple portal at Delphi, as testimony to a basic truth to be adopted as a minimal norm by those who seek to set themselves apart from the rest of creation as 'human beings', that is as those who 'know themselves'."[1]

Acquiring self-knowledge, however, is a slow and painful process, which is the reason people tend to avoid it. We have a psychological defense mechanism known as denial, which helps us to avoid owning up to our personality weaknesses by denying the reality of our problems or by blaming them on others. Thus, Jesus asked the rhetorical question "Why do you see the speck that is in your brother's eye, but do not notice the log that is in your own eye?" (Mt 7:3).

Because of our natural love for and loyalty to our parents, we also tend to deny problems in our family of origin and the link between our parents and our personality weaknesses. Yet uncovering the behaviors that we modeled after our parents can help us to obtain self-knowledge. We can then be both grateful for the good things we learned from them and vigilant to remedy the bad things.

Modeling

Modeling after parents begins early in one's life, most often without one's awareness. We are all familiar with the saying "monkey see, monkey do." Over the last two decades,

---

[1] John Paul II, Encyclical Letter *Fides et ratio* (September 14, 1998), no. 1.

neuroscience research has been investigating whether imitating the behavior of others, particularly the behavior of one's parents, has a physiological basis. One view is that the process of modeling after a parent is possibly mediated via the mirror neuron system in the brain. Whatever scientists might discover, clinical experience indicates that modeling is a powerful psychological mechanism that influences our personality development and the ways we relate to others, particularly the people with whom we are most vulnerable, such as a spouse and children.

The process of modeling after parents is so powerful that people find themselves imitating the bad behaviors that they vowed never to repeat. I have treated many spouses who had made a decision not to repeat a parent's bad temper or controlling behavior but then later found themselves doing the very thing they had intended to avoid. They can say with Saint Paul, "I do not do the good I want, but the evil I do not want is what I do" (Rom 7:19).

Fortunately, parental weaknesses acquired through modeling can be resolved through the hard work of understanding and forgiving the parent who disappointed or hurt us. Only then can we make a fruitful commitment to grow in the good habits that can conquer those weaknesses.

Parent Traits Survey

An effective way to become aware of the behaviors one has modeled after each parent is to take the following survey. (You may photocopy this survey if you do not want to write in the book.) In the left column are personality strengths that are essential to a healthy marriage. In the right column are weaknesses that harm the capacity for self-giving love.

I. Your Father

Rate your father regarding how he related to your mother with the good habits in the left column and the weaknesses in the right column. Write 1 for rarely, 2 for periodically, and 3 for often.

Loving & Affectionate ___	Emotionally Distant ___
Generous ___	Selfish ___
Forgiving ___	Angry ___
Respectful ___	Controlling ___
Trusting & Calm ___	Anxious & Irritable ___
Hopeful & Cheerful ___	Sad & Negative ___
Confident & Positive ___	Insecure & Withdrawn ___
Verbally Supportive & Upbeat ___	Perfectionistic & Critical ___
	Immature & Weak ___
Mature & Strong ___	Lack of Prudence or Life
Healthy Priorities ___	Balance ___

Identify good habits that you may have acquired from your father.

1.

2.

3.

Identify weaknesses you may have acquired from your father.

1.

2.

3.

II. Your Mother

Rate your mother regarding how she related to your father with the good habits in the left column and the weaknesses in the right column. Mark 1 for rarely, 2 for periodically, and 3 for often.

Loving & Affectionate ___	Emotionally Distant ___
Generous ___	Selfish ___
Forgiving ___	Angry ___
Respectful ___	Controlling ___
Trusting & Calm ___	Anxious & Irritable ___
Hopeful & Cheerful ___	Sad & Negative ___
Confident & Positive ___	Insecure & Withdrawn ___
Verbally Supportive & Upbeat ___	Perfectionistic & Critical ___
Mature & Strong ___	Immature & Weak ___
Healthy Priorities ___	Lack of Prudence or Life Balance ___

Identify good habits you may have acquired from your mother.

1.

2.

3.

Identify weaknesses you may have acquired from your mother.

1.

2.

3.

III. Both Parents

Reflect on the ways both parents have had an impact on you with the following questions.

1. Which parent helped you more? _____

2. Which parent disappointed you more? _____

3. Do you think that the parent who disappointed you more was modeling after

    __ his or her father?

    __ his or her mother?

4. Do you think that this parent was influenced by

    __ life stresses?

    __ marital conflicts?

Your Spouse

Since the majority of psychological conflicts in marriage arise from unresolved issues in the spouses' family of origin, spouses have a responsibility to know not only their own background but also that of the other spouse, hence the following question:

How do you think your spouse's strengths and weaknesses from his or her parents may be influencing your marriage?

List some positive ways.

1.
2.
3.

List some negative ways.
1.
2.
3.

Review and Reflection

Spouses with low levels of conflict report the benefit of reviewing this survey together and discussing the strengths and the weaknesses they have brought into their marriages. In those with higher levels of conflict, the focus first needs to be on the core goodness of each spouse, followed by discussions about one or two acquired parental weaknesses at a time. The point of the exercise is for the spouses to be grateful for the good traits they have acquired from their parents, to forgive their weaknesses, and to resolve to overcome learned negative traits.

While reviewing the survey, it helps for spouses to keep in mind that unless they forgive their parents' faults and failures, they are likely to misdirect anger from the past at their spouses or children without realizing it. Unresolved hurts often cause a person to be an emotional prisoner of the past.

Also worth considering is that children who do not feel safe with both their parents are likely to grow up with difficulty in trusting others, especially a future spouse. Similarly, children who did not feel close to both parents often struggle with loneliness, sadness, anxiety, and anger as adults. The good news is that by working on forgiving parents, one can decrease current emotional pain that has its roots in the past. It helps to know that although father wounds are more common, mother wounds are sometimes more difficult to resolve because the secure attachment to the mother is more essential to a child's ability to feel safe in life and, subsequently, to give and to receive love, trust, and praise.

Adult Children of Addicted Parents

The emotional trauma from growing up with a substance-abusing parent damages a child's basic ability to trust. Childhood memories of fear, sadness, and anger toward an addicted parent can reemerge in marriage and lead to emotional overreactions. These can include controlling behaviors, excessive anger, and periodic intense sadness, particularly at Thanksgiving and Christmas, when the lack of family harmony and togetherness is most keenly felt.

A commitment to forgiving addicted parents can decrease the emotional pain caused by episodes in the past and can help spouses to grow in hope for their own marriages. As they look for the goodness in their wounded parents, they can also grow in trust.

The Impact of Parental Divorce

The process of review and reflection should require acknowledging the pain caused by the divorce of one's parents. The sad reality is that the divorce epidemic has contributed to an intergenerational cycle of divorce. Specifically, adults whose parents divorced are 89 percent more likely to divorce, compared with adults who were raised in intact families. Children of divorce who marry other children of divorce have an even higher risk of ending up divorced.[2]

[2] Nicholas H. Wolfinger, *Understanding the Divorce Cycle: The Children of Divorce in Their Own Marriages* (New York: Cambridge University Press, 2005), 74.

Difficulty in maintaining trust in loving relationships has been repeatedly identified as a major weakness in the adult children of divorce, and unless it is addressed, it can undermine their future marriages. This weakness is often unconscious and sometimes emerges only after many years of married life. If it does, adult children of divorce need the assurance that they do not have to be the prisoners of their past trauma but can find freedom through forgiveness and growth in trust.

The Influence of Siblings and Peers

As relationships with parents affect personality development, so do relationships with siblings. In a Harvard Medical School study of childhood sibling relationships as a predictor of major depression, 229 men revealed that poorer relationships with siblings prior to age twenty and a family history of depression independently predicted both the occurrence of major depression and the frequency of use of mood-altering drugs by age fifty.[3]

Some spouses bring into their marriages wounds received from broken friendships or romantic relationships. As with family members, forgiveness of offenders and gratitude for God-given gifts are essential for resolving wounds from the past. Here faith can be helpful.

Abortion Trauma

As described in the first chapter, abortion trauma can later have negative consequences in a marriage. It can particularly

---

[3] Robert J. Waldinger, George E. Vaillant, and E. John Orav, "Childhood Sibling Relationships as a Predictor of Major Depression in Adulthood: A 30-Year Prospective Study", *American Journal of Psychiatry* 164, no. 6 (June 2007): 949–54, http://doi.org/10.1176/ajp.2007.164.6.949.

harm the ability to trust a spouse and can subsequently result in overreactions of anger and in emotionally distant and controlling behaviors. Although this is a very sensitive issue to address, it needs to be uncovered for healing to take place. Ideally, the couple should participate in a post-abortion healing program, such as Project Rachel.

While spouses and engaged persons often fear that admitting a past abortion may endanger the relationship, my experience has been that such honesty, in fact, strengthens the relationship. An understanding response often requires forgiving the transgression. If the abortion occurred in the relationship of the couple, mutual requests for forgiveness and the Sacrament of Reconciliation are essential to healing the emotional wound.

Humility Needed for Uncovering and Addressing Weaknesses

Humility involves accepting the whole truth about ourselves. This means recognizing strengths as well as limitations and weaknesses. Humility is the virtue that overcomes our pride and defense mechanisms so that we can admit our conflicts and do something about them. Humility also helps us to overcome the tendency to blame others, especially our spouses, for marital conflicts.

Saint Thomas Aquinas defined humility as "seeing ourselves as God sees us, knowing that every good we have comes from him as pure gift". He described the two ways a person can grow in humility: "First and chiefly by a gift of grace, and in this way the inner man precedes the outward man. The other way is by human effort, whereby he first of all restrains the outward man and afterwards succeeds in plucking out the inward root."[4]

---

[4] Thomas Aquinas, *Summa theologica* II-II, q. 161, art. 6.

For real progress, we must admit that we are powerless over ourselves without the help of God, and this too is an act of humility. Humility also helps us to restrain the tendency to expect perfection from ourselves and others, which is really a form of pride. To help with this, we must remind ourselves that there has been only one perfect family, the Holy Family. Meditating on Scripture passages such as the following can help us to accept compassionately the truth about ourselves, our parents, and our spouses:

> My son, perform your tasks in meekness;
>> then you will be loved more than a giver of gifts.
> The greater you are, the more you must humble yourself;
>> so you will find favor with God.
> There are many who are noble and renowned,
>> but it is to the humble that he reveals his mysteries....
> Seek not what is too difficult for you,
>> nor investigate what is beyond your power.
> Reflect upon what has been assigned to you.
>
> (Sir 3:17–19, 21–22)

> What does the LORD require of you but to do justice, and to love kindness, and to walk humbly with your God?
>
> (Mic 6:8)

> Judge not, that you be not judged. For with the judgment you pronounce you will be judged, and the measure you give will be the measure you get.
>
> (Mt 7:1–2)

An Ongoing Process

Spouses soon learn that growing in self-knowledge is an ongoing process. Time with extended family can often provide new insights into family-of-origin weaknesses.

After spending a holiday with in-laws, for example, one may notice for the first time how a spouse is repeating a negative trait modeled after a parent. Some people often relate that only after many years of marriage do they come to discover in their spouses, often to their surprise, a negative parental weakness, such as being critical, mistrustful, controlling, or distant.

When one becomes aware of a family weakness in one's spouse that is creating stress in the marriage, it needs to be discussed in a loving, gentle manner. I recommend that the spouse pointing out the problem first communicate a negative trait of his own. Only then should that spouse gently and respectfully request, "Honey, I think our friendship would be helped if you also addressed a weakness that I have come to see in your parent that you may be repeating in our marriage." The couple will need to develop a plan together to protect the marriage from these learned behaviors.

The Role of Faith

Growth in self-knowledge is a challenging, lifelong process. Many couples report that their faith is essential for helping them to identify and to work on these character weaknesses. Catholic spouses might find the following exercises helpful in their quest to know and love themselves and each other:

- Praying, "Lord, reveal to me any weaknesses that I may have acquired from my parents."
- Praying, "Lord, help me to repeat the good qualities of my parents but not their weaknesses, such as _____."

- Praying, "Lord, deepen my trust in you with our marriage and my trust in my spouse."
- Examining one's conscience daily
- Admitting powerlessness over weaknesses daily and turning them over to the Lord
- Giving to the Lord any anger arising from hurts from one's parents
- Praying for growth in humility and in other specific virtues
- Meditating on Christ in the Gospels
- Meditating on Saint Joseph and asking for his intercession
- Meditating on the life of the Blessed Mother, for example by praying the Rosary

If a spouse is unwilling to grow in self-knowledge, prayer for humility can be helpful. Since, in the Sacrament of Marriage, spouses are no longer two but one, such prayer offered by the open spouse is often effective in reducing the fear that might be blocking growth in self-knowledge in the other spouse.

Growth in self-knowledge can also be encouraged through participating in a marriage enrichment program, seeking guidance from a mentor couple, and receiving counsel from a mental health professional who values the Catholic Sacrament of Marriage.

The recognition of the importance of the Sacrament of Marriage, to both the spouses and their children, motivates Catholic husbands and wives to engage in the hard work of uncovering their conflicts, identifying their sources, and overcoming them with the power of grace. This process is, in fact, the calling of every Christian—to grow in virtue with the help of God. And it is worked out in the lives of married Christians in their relationships with one another.

Meanwhile, the knowledge of the good habits that spouses have acquired from their parents can strengthen their confidence and hope. There is every reason to be optimistic that the work of redemption that the Lord has begun in their lives will be brought to completion.

RESOURCES

Books

Anderson, Carl, and José Granados. *Called to Love: Approaching John Paul II's Theology of the Body.* New York: Image Books, 2009.

Chapman, Gary. *The Five Love Languages: How to Express Heartfelt Commitment to Your Mate.* Chicago: Northfield, 2015.

Dodaro, Robert, O.S.A., ed. *Remaining in the Truth of Christ: Marriage and Communion in the Catholic Church.* San Francisco: Ignatius Press, 2017.

John Paul II, Apostolic Exhortation on the Role of the Christian Family in the Modern World *Familiaris consortio* (November 22, 1981).

———. *Man and Woman He Created Them: A Theology of the Body.* Translated by Michael Waldstein. Boston: Pauline Books, 2006.

———. Letter to Families *Gratissimam sane* (February 2, 1994).

———. *Letter to Women* (June 29, 1995).

McCarthy, Margaret, ed. *Torn Asunder: Children, the Myth of the Good Divorce and the Recovery of Origins.* Grand Rapids: Eerdmans, 2017.

Miller, Leila, ed. *Primal Loss: The Now Adult Children of Divorce Speak.* Phoenix: LCB Publishing, 2017.

Olmstead, Thomas, *Complete My Joy: Apostolic Exhortation to Husbands and Wives, Mothers and Fathers of the Diocese of Phoenix* (December 30, 2018).

Pontifical Council for the Family. *The Truth and Meaning of Human Sexuality: Guidelines for Education within the Family* (December 8, 1995).

Sheen, Fulton J. *Three to Get Married*. Princeton, N.J.: Scepter Publishers, 1996.

Spinelli, Richard. *Understanding Love and Responsibility*. Boston: Pauline Books and Media, 2004.

Websites

The Alexander House (www.thealexanderhouse.org)
The Alexander House offers Catholic parish-based marital enrichment programs.

Child Healing (www.childhealing.com)
My website Child Healing uncovers and addresses psychological conflicts in children and adolescents.

National Marriage Project (www.nationalmarriageproject
.org)
The National Marriage Project provides research and analysis on the health of marriage in America, analyzes the social and cultural forces shaping contemporary marriage, and identifies strategies to increase marital quality and stability.

Retrouvaille (www.retrouvaille.org)
This program offers couples the tools they need to rediscover a loving marriage relationship.